The Trainer's Tool Kit

Cy Charney
and
Kathy Conway

AMACOM
American Management Association

New York • Atlanta • Boston • Chicago • Kansas City • San Francisco • Washington, D.C.
Brussels • Mexico City • Tokyo • Toronto

*This publication is designed to provide accurate and authoritative
information in regard to the subject matter covered. It is sold with the
understanding that the publisher is not engaged in rendering legal,
accounting, or other professional service. If legal advice or other expert
assistance is required, the services of a competent professional person
should be sought.*

Library of Congress Cataloging-in-Publication Data

Charney, Cyril.
    The trainer's tool kit / Cy Charney and Kathy Conway.
        p.   cm.
    Includes indexes.
    ISBN 0-8144-7944-8
        *1. Employees—Training of—Handbooks, manuals, etc.   I. Conway,
Kathy.   II. Title.*
    HF5549.5.T7C5412   1997
    658.3'124—dc21   *97-23134*
                                                               CIP

Printing number

10   9   8   7   6   5   4   3   2

To my wife,
Rhona Charney

To my husband,
Peter Janecek

Contents

Preface and Acknowledgments

This book is intended to help line managers and professional trainers improve the effectiveness of their training and development activities. Why aim the book at this double audience? Simple. Our observations are that although professional trainers will always have a valuable place in the corporate world, the pendulum is swinging dramatically toward making line people more accountable for training staff.

Take a look at what people in a position of authority do today. They facilitate, coach, and train. They are spending less time managing the details and more time overseeing the process. They get people involved in finding new, ingenious ways of adding value to customers. They are not the technical experts; they hire and train people to become proficient in those tasks.

So what would we call someone doing this day in and day out? A "coach" or "leader" would be a better description than "manager" or "supervisor." Such a person would spend time developing others to take increased responsibility through the acquisition of additional skills and knowledge—technical, business, and interpersonal. Who can do this? Can we leave it all to human resources? Clearly the answer is no. The responsibility will fall increasingly on the shoulders of line people.

And how do these changes affect those who are managing the training function? To be sure they are being called on to do more with less. They probably have fewer resources in terms of full-time trainers, and they need to do more training themselves, outsource more, and find other economical ways of delivering training through the use of technology and by the initiative of the learners themselves.

In this new environment, their skill-set will change. They need to have classroom savvy and the basic skills of training adults if they are doing more work in the classroom. They need to be able to organize and coordinate programs using consultants and need to know how to select, negotiate, and develop partnerships with consultants.

Finally, they need to know about the new technologies that appear almost daily. And trainers need to know how to provide people with the necessary tools so that they can become more self-directed and less dependent on the training department for skills acquisition.

This book is aimed at providing effective tools for the challenge of developing people, whether this task is done by line managers or professional trainers brought in from outside the organization. By organizing the information into short "how-to" topics, full of practical ideas, we have made this book a quick reference guide instead of a book that you might read from cover to cover once only.

We want to thank a number of people who served conscientiously on our editorial committee, acting as a sounding board for ideas and providing valuable practical insight into this important subject:

Marybeth Ashbourne, Holt Renfrew
Malcolm Bernstein, Geller, Shedletsky & Weiss
Adrian Carter, Nesbitt Burns Ltd.
Dianne Conrad, University of Alberta
Graham Crawford, Gilmore & Associates
Kimberly Davis, Chase Manhattan Bank
Dennis Eaton, management consultant
Birgitte Hohn, Industry Canada
Judy McLeod, AT&T Long Distance Services
Lynda Mitchell, Sun Media
Linda Mulhall, Toronto Board of Education
Gregg Murtagh, Sectorial Skills Council
Shirley Spring, Criminal Injury Compensation, Workers' Compensation Board of British Columbia
Gladys Winkworth, Rochester Institute of Technology
Robin Winn, Saville Systems

Other people who contributed to the content were Filalete Monteiro, Sylvie Mui, Deborah Nelson, Bob Power, Rich (Richard) Filler, and Daneal Charney.

We thank Rosemary Kercz, who provided meticulous editing and word processing support for the project.

Adult Learning Principles

A dult training needs to be done quite differently from the way we were trained as children.

- You will be more successful at training if you remember that adults:
    - ✓ Want to learn. They realize that training is a key to their performance and their success. In a world where layoffs are commonplace, people realize that the one thing they can take with them to a new job and career is their skills.
    - ✓ Need to be involved and consulted. Letting them know what will be learned, by whom, and when it will be done will increase the buy-in and the commitment to participate enthusiastically.
    - ✓ Want to feel that the content is relevant. They need to feel that the materials have been designed with their special circumstances in mind.
    - ✓ Like to be able to challenge the content and process. Adults need to feel that they can critique ideas frankly.
    - ✓ Enjoy being able to ask questions. The issues that they raise need to be treated seriously and dealt with in an agreed-upon time.
    - ✓ Like to be treated as equals. No one likes to be talked down to or treated as a child.
    - ✓ Want to be able to practice in a risk-free environment.
    - ✓ Appreciate feedback on how they are doing. Without appropriate validation of their behavior, they may not develop the confidence to repeat the skills that they have learned or correct the skills they performed incorrectly.
    - ✓ Listen actively, confirming the ideas that they agree with and challenging those they disagree with
    - ✓ Need to be challenged. They should be given tasks that will make them think and behave in ways that will require them to stretch.

- ✓ Learn differently and work at different rates, because of each person's unique experience, background, ability, and learning styles.
- ✓ May need to unlearn old ideas and habits before they can learn something new.
- ✓ Need to build on their own experiences and knowledge.
- ✓ Are interested in seeking practical solutions to their problems.
- People remember concepts they:
  - ✓ Learned most recently.
  - ✓ Heard about more than once.
  - ✓ Were able to practice.
  - ✓ Could implement right away.
  - ✓ Understand are important to know and use.
  - ✓ Are encouraged or rewarded for using by their manger or other important people in the organization.

Alternatives to Training

A coach's objective is to find the fastest, most economical method of closing a knowledge or skill gap. Do an up-front needs analysis to make sure that training is the answer.

- Training cannot close a skill gap that is caused by:
  - ✓ Poor morale or attitude.
  - ✓ Poor policies or procedures.
  - ✓ Equipment problems.
  - ✓ Lack of incentives.
- Training may not be the fastest solution for closing a skill gap when:
  - ✓ The time to develop and deliver the training cannot meet new skill implementation deadlines.
  - ✓ Employee time off the job to attend training will result in decreased productivity.
  - ✓ Work shifts and holiday schedules necessitate training small groups at a time, over a long period of time.
- Training may not be the most economical solution for closing a skill gap when:
  - ✓ There are only a few employees affected by a new skill requirement.
  - ✓ The need for new skills is only short term.
  - ✓ Costs of a course are higher than the benefits the training will produce.
  - ✓ Regular training courses are poorly attended.
  - ✓ Courses convey information only, not skill building.
- Here are some alternatives to training for closing skill gaps:
  - ✓ Change hiring and promotion criteria to reflect new skill requirements.
  - ✓ Pay higher salaries for some positions to attract job-ready employees.
  - ✓ Institute job-shadowing programs.
  - ✓ Set up formal mentor programs.

✓ Implement job rotations for hands-on practical experience.

✓ Set up buddy systems with retired employees.

✓ Recognize and reward managers who are effective coaches.

✓ Set up individual development plans for employees whose performance is unsatisfactory.

✓ Create "self-service" employee learning resource centers, which provide training materials that people can borrow.

✓ Develop user-friendly, self-paced, how-to manuals and job aids for common problems.

✓ Establish help lines for equipment- and technology-related problems.

✓ Designate experienced employees as troubleshooters for specialized problems.

✓ Put together a list of employees with specialized skills and training who can provide individual assistance.

✓ Hold cross-functional meetings for employees to share their expertise.

✓ Set aside time in regular meetings for employees to brainstorm problems and coping techniques.

✓ Invite industry experts to participate in information panels.

✓ Design a tuition reimbursement program for job-related education.

✓ Reimburse employee purchases of job-related books and videos.

- Training is especially ineffective and expensive when it is used:

   —To train large groups of people in order to correct the behavior of only a few.

   —To inspire or motivate employees. Only good management practices and meaningful compensation strategies can do that.

   —To correct fundamental hiring errors.

   —To encourage employees to market or sell products that the customers don't want.

   —To solve disciplinary problems. These are one-on-one situations.

   —To reduce employee turnover or absenteeism. Working conditions are usually the culprit here.

- Employee input and feedback is often the best source of suggestions for cost-effective alternatives to expensive training. Put their resourcefulness to work for you.

Benchmarking

Benchmarking allows you to compare your practices, such as training, with those of acknowledged industry leaders in order to identify opportunities for your organization to improve.

- There are three types of benchmarking that apply to training practices:
  - ✓ Internal benchmarking: Comparing training costs and practices in one division or location to another within a company
  - ✓ Competitive benchmarking: Comparing training costs and practices to companies in your industry
  - ✓ Generic benchmarking: Comparing training costs and practices with companies outside your industry
- Benchmarking best practices in training can refer to:
  - ✓ Organizationwide training practices and costs.
  - ✓ Training department practices and costs.
- Benchmarking organizationwide training practices and costs can examine:
  - ✓ Annual training costs per employee.
  - ✓ Annual training days per employee.
  - ✓ Total annual training costs represented as a percentage of total annual salary costs.
  - ✓ Salaries of training department staff represented as a percentage of total salaries in the company.
  - ✓ Ratio of training department staff to total staff.
  - ✓ Training evaluation and measurement tools.
  - ✓ Training planning and budgeting practices.
- There are seven key steps for using benchmarking to improve your costs and effectiveness:
  - ✓ Choose the processes to be benchmarked.
  - ✓ Select and train the benchmarking team.
  - ✓ Select the right partner.
  - ✓ Analyze your own process.
  - ✓ Gather data from all appropriate sources.

✓ Identify the gaps between your processes and those recognized as "best practices."
✓ Develop a plan for improvement.
✓ Implement the required changes.
- Training practices can be difficult to benchmark because companies differ radically in their expectations for training. However, by identifying some key processes, comparing your practices to companies with similar challenges, and following the seven key steps in benchmarking, you can bring a better business focus to your training.

Here are some guidelines for implementing each of the key steps.

Step One: Choose Processes to Be Benchmarked

✓ Interview key customer groups to understand what is important to them with respect to training outcomes.
✓ Analyze the major costs of your training department and training programs to the company.
✓ Clarify the key goals and objectives for a training department in the overall company business plan.
✓ Prioritize one or two practices as areas for improvement.
✓ Identify specific improvements you hope to achieve.

Step Two: Select and Train the Benchmarking Team

✓ Put together a cross-functional team with representatives from key customer groups.
✓ Include both management and nonmanagement representatives to give the team the advantage of different perspectives.
✓ Choose team members who are enthusiastic about change.
✓ Ensure that team members have a basic understanding of the processes being examined.
✓ Include a senior person, capable of authorizing changes.

Step Three: Select the Right Partner

- ✓ Consulting firms may have a database on leading organizations and best practices.
- ✓ Your network of professional associates might be able to identify leaders in the area you have chosen.
- ✓ Government agencies and industry associations are helpful for information gathering.
- ✓ As a rule of thumb, consider companies of similar size as your benchmarks for training practices.

Step Four: Analyze Your Own Processes

- ✓ Measure both inputs and outputs of a training process.
- ✓ Use factual data such as time, costs, and employee time.
- ✓ Use flowcharts to identify process components.

Step Five: Gather Data

- If you conduct research through visits to other organizations:
  - ✓ Get permission from a person in that organization with the necessary power to make such a decision.
  - ✓ Be clear about the information you require and the time the visit will take. Have your team prepare a list of the information it is seeking.
  - ✓ Offer reciprocal help and information in return for the organization's cooperation.
  - ✓ Some "best practices" companies charge fees for site visits. Establish if this is the case for your host companies.
  - ✓ Gather additional information as may be required through:
    —Networking at conferences.
    —Interviewing employees who have worked at these organizations previously.
    —Trade associations.
    —The Internet (home pages, chat groups).
    —Trade journals.

Step Six: Identify Gaps

✓ Compare "best practices" data with your company data.
✓ Determine which variables are within your control for effecting change.
✓ Clarify the benefits the organization will gain by closing the gap.

Step Seven: Develop a Plan for Improvement

✓ Document an action plan that contains:
  —The steps to be taken.
  —Who will be responsible for each step.
  —When each step will be completed.
  —Who might need to be informed about the plan.

Step Eight: Implement the Changes

✓ Set realistic deadlines for implementation.
✓ Develop a clear communication plan about the change implementation.
✓ Be very clear about the cooperation and approvals you require from others in your company.
✓ Issue regular progress reports.
✓ Ask your customers to evaluate your results.
✓ Be prepared to amend your plan as business conditions change.

Budgeting for Training

Too often training plans and budgets sit on a shelf as circumstances and priorities change. Training that does take place may have little to do with what was planned. When training budgets are ignored, training's relationship to the success of the organization may be questioned.

Here are some ways in which training budgets and plans can be taken seriously:

- Break budget projections into four key categories:
  - ✓ *Organization skill gaps:* Training that supports mandatory changes in the business plan, including new products, services, and technology
  - ✓ *Turnover gaps:* Training that supports employee orientation to the organization or to a new business unit
  - ✓ *Individual skill gaps:* Training that is unique to an individual's performance
  - ✓ *Strategic change gaps:* Training to facilitate a new direction or to promote a change in culture
- When these skill gaps have been identified, do the following analyses:
  - ✓ Differentiate between "must do" and "nice to do" priorities.
  - ✓ Establish the total budget commitment for each category.
  - ✓ Determine the total amount of employee time off the job that can be guaranteed for training purposes.
  - ✓ Determine the best training courses or tools that will fit the dollar and time allocations for priority skill gaps.
  - ✓ Add to the costs of courses the costs of trainee travel, training facilities, and printed resource material.
  - ✓ Allocate a contingency cost for unexpected business plan changes. Use a guideline of 10 percent of the total of the above costs.

- You must understand business plans *before* developing your own plan for training. Linking the two will provide the greatest benefit to the organization.
- To research the best method for budget projections for your organization, consider the following sources:
  - ✓ Competitor research
  - ✓ Companies with the same employee base
  - ✓ Government research
  - ✓ Industry and association research
  - ✓ Recruitment plans
  - ✓ Retirement projections
  - ✓ Product upgrades
  - ✓ Equipment upgrades
- Before building detailed training plans, determine the maximum amount of resources your organization will invest, keeping in mind all of the considerations outlined above.
- Here are some of the most common methods used to scope out training budgets for direct training costs:
  - ✓ Commit a set percentage for training based on overall salary expenditures.
  - ✓ Commit a set percentage for training based on overall anticipated organization revenue.
  - ✓ Establish a standard number of days per employee for professional development.
  - ✓ Prioritize training needs that are articulated in the business plan, and estimate the associated costs.
  - ✓ Use historical information about training costs. Adjust these costs for inflation and changes in the number of employees.
  - ✓ Total all cost estimates submitted by individual line managers.
  - ✓ Subtract the current figure for all salaries from the total amount of salaries that would be owing if all employees were paid at the maximum allowable level.
  - ✓ Use figures from government agencies and professional associations to set your organization's guidelines.
- The grid shown in Exhibit 1 can be used to reexamine your costs and anticipated benefits and perhaps to realign monies and delivery options.

Exhibit 1. Training cost grid.

Training Solution	Priority Ranking	(A) Number of Participants	(B) Length of Course	(C) Total Training Time (A) × (B)	(D) Cost per Participant Day (includes materials and instruction)	(E) Total Participant Cost (C) × (D)	(F) Total Facilities Cost	(G) Total Travel Cost	Total Cost (E) + (F) + (G)
Leadership training	1	250	2	500	100	$ 50,000	$ 4,000	25 × $500 = $12,500	$ 66,500
Time management training	2	1,000	1	1,000	150	$150,000	$ 2,000	Ø	$152,000
Multimedia equipment overview	3	20	1	20	500	$ 10,000	Ø	Ø	$ 10,000
Introduction to sales and marketing	4	300	2	600	50	$ 30,000	In-house facilities	Ø	$ 30,000

- The grid shown in Exhibit 2 can be used to help you identify your most urgent training needs when considering the best training solutions to meet those needs.

The largest expenditure in this fictitious company is committed to time management training. Although there is a relatively low cost per participant, the anticipated trainee population creates a very large expense. Perhaps only one-quarter of the target population should attend; they can become coaches and mentors if funds run short. Similarly, the "Introduction to Sales and Marketing" item might be conducted through a lower-cost video and supporting workbook.

Exhibit 2. Training priority grid.

Training Need	Skill Gap (check one—X)			Business Impact (check one—X)			Priority Ranking	Training Solution
	Low	Med.	High	Low	Med.	High		

Example:

Training Need	Training Solution	Skill Gap (check one—X)			Business Impact (check one—X)			Priority Ranking
		A	B	C	3	2	1	
Orientation Training for 25 newly recruited sales reps	Product Overview Training		X			X		2
Management Training for 10 new supervisors	Corporate Leadership Program		X		X			1
Customer Service Training for Technicians	Purchase XYZ course from KLM vendor	X					X	3

(In this chart, the reasons for the rankings are as follows for this fictitious company:)

The liability of untrained supervisors is considered the greatest need because of their inexperience and their effect on employee morale. Although the product knowledge for sales reps is a mandatory requirement, there are other methods available for them to learn the products—brochures and access to seasoned sales reps. The customer service training for technicians is a new business opportunity that will enhance the company's public relations profile, with a long-term objective of increasing sales.

Although each training project has important impact on business, it is critical to differentiate the magnitude of each impact.

Budgets: Building a Case for More Training Dollars

Most organizations today find themselves in a catch-22 situation about training:

- An increase in the amount of training required to meet changing market conditions over time as employees need more and diverse skills.
- A decrease in funding that organizations can invest in the long-term benefits of training due to short-term budget restrictions.

- Making a case for more training dollars requires research and data from many sources. A comprehensive analysis about the requirement for more training dollars should focus on the following:
  - ✓ Business plan liabilities
  - ✓ Benchmarking
  - ✓ Customer and employee feedback

Business Plan Liabilities

- Your organization's twelve-month business plan will outline key initiatives that are critical to its success. Many of these initiatives assume the availability of competent and trained staff. The business plan can be jeopardized if staff are not trained in such areas as:
  - ✓ New equipment startup.
  - ✓ New or enhanced information technology.
  - ✓ Maintenance and repair of older equipment.
  - ✓ Features and benefits of new products.

✓ Updated research about customer attitudes and expectations.

✓ New legislation affecting manufacturing processes, safety standards, workplace conditions, and employee relations.

- Prepare a situation analysis that describes the current operating capability for meeting these new requirements. Any skills shortfall that is not in the training plan should be highlighted, costed, and presented to management as a key condition for meeting planning projections.
- In any operating environment, there are other liabilities attached to limiting training. These risks are often not seen as training issues—until it's too late. Be on the lookout for these signals:

  ✓ Unusually high staff turnover, often caused by inexperienced or untrained managers

  ✓ Delays in meeting customer delivery deadlines

  ✓ Customer complaints about product defects and not meeting service standards

  ✓ Equipment breakdown

  ✓ Billing mistakes and invoicing errors

  ✓ Missed production targets

- Training is not the solution for all of these problems, but there may be a relationship between training and performance standards in past records. In documenting these relationships, compare the costs of inefficiencies to the costs of training, and set priorities for using training dollars where the benefits clearly outweigh the costs.
- Be sure to include an analysis of the availability of qualified, trained staff to replace employees who leave. External recruiting and on-site orientation are expensive.

Benchmarking

- Draw on the many sources of information that can help you to determine a reasonable training investment for your organization. Gathering this information should be an ongoing activity. Here are some sources that you can access readily:

  ✓ Professional training associations that provide data about training costs, broken down by organization size and type

- ✓ Government agencies that collect data about industrywide training expenditures (training costs, training days, etc.)
- ✓ Industry and trade associations, which often conduct surveys to benchmark training costs
- ✓ Your own organization. With a little research you can analyze annual changes to the training budget and compare them to changes in employee population and business plan achievement.
- ✓ Consultants who work with your company, who often have interesting observations about overall trends for training investments
- When presenting your research, be sure to include all associated costs of training:
  - ✓ Training staff salaries
  - ✓ Multimedia equipment
  - ✓ Outsourcing
  - ✓ Reference materials
  - ✓ Travel and accommodation costs
- Break down all associated costs, and pinpoint which ones can contribute to greater efficiencies and economies of scale.

Customer and Employee Feedback

- Customer and employee feedback can provide compelling evidence for the need for increased training investments. Use the following tools to gather meaningful feedback and ongoing needs analyses:
  - ✓ Employee attitude surveys
  - ✓ Information about training practices and needs gained during exit interviews
  - ✓ Records to help you track the number of employees hired externally that occurred over a period of time due to a lack of qualified internal candidates
  - ✓ Employee focus groups
  - ✓ Customer focus groups
  - ✓ Customer complaint logs
  - ✓ Customer satisfaction surveys
  - ✓ Feedback from sales and customer service representatives

Career Planning Programs

The training investment that organizations make is maximized when employees can link their own goals to business goals.

- Career development for employees in an organization can take many forms:
  - ✓ Increased responsibility and enhanced skill sets in a current job
  - ✓ A lateral move to another position
  - ✓ Advancement to a higher level
  - ✓ Long-term planning for a career change
  - ✓ Reduced responsibilities for lifestyle priorities
  - ✓ Retraining for new and emerging occupations
- Companies that establish a clear relationship between training and career development enjoy these benefits:
  - ✓ A competitive advantage in attracting new employees
  - ✓ A better ability to retain employees
  - ✓ Increased employee morale and motivation
  - ✓ Meaningful succession planning
  - ✓ Business plans that identify realistic objectives for employee development
- Here are some of the most common ways organizations promote individual responsibility for career planning:
  - ✓ The provision of standardized career planning seminars available to all employees—either mandatory or voluntary attendance, during or outside normal business hours
  - ✓ Career planning workbooks for use during seminars or as stand-alone aids
  - ✓ Self-help books, videos, or computer-based tools for self-directed study

- ✓ The establishment of a formal mentor program with clear roles and responsibilities for both mentors and mentees
- An effective career planning seminar, workbook, or computer-based training aid should address the following elements:
  - ✓ Emphasis on individual accountability for career management
  - ✓ Up-to-date information about the competitive marketplace and the customer base
  - ✓ Self-assessment exercises about skills and personal preferences
  - ✓ Personal marketing techniques
  - ✓ Information-gathering techniques
  - ✓ Developing mentor relationships
  - ✓ Comprehensive information about company-supported training
  - ✓ The relationship of continuous learning to corporate objectives
  - ✓ The importance of identifying hidden success factors: adapting to change, coping with stress, and helping others be successful
  - ✓ Cost-effectiveness
  - ✓ Accessibility for all employees, including employees at different geographic locations and those who work shifts
- Career planning programs work best when:
  - ✓ Senior management supports the program.
  - ✓ There is a role for managers to support and reinforce the objectives of the program.
  - ✓ There are self-study tools for employees to use for their personal development and growth.

Case Studies

A case study is a description of a realistic work situation that highlights a problem. The problem can be resolved in a variety of ways, using principles and theory given earlier to the trainee.

- Case studies are typically documented in writing, but can be in video format too.
- Analysis and problem solving can be done individually, in groups, or combined (individually, then comparing answers in groups).
- A good case study:
  - ✓ Covers one area of theory.
  - ✓ Is intellectually challenging.
  - ✓ Is realistic.
  - ✓ Is customized to suit the audience in terms of its description of the organization, products, customers, culture, and other factors.
  - ✓ Provides adequate time to enable detailed analysis and discussion.
- The logical order of using case studies is as follows:
  1. Hand out the case study.
  2. Review the steps you will be taking and the time allowance. Check for understanding.
  3. Allow time for people to read the material.
  4. Allow people to read the questions individually and make notes on their answers. This will challenge everyone to think before the group discussion.
  5. Set up groups to analyze the case. This can be done by randomly counting off people and having everyone with the same number work together, or by trying to mix people up so that the greatest variety of personalities and backgrounds are together. (Homogeneous groups learn less and finish quickly.)
  6. Appoint a facilitator in each group of four to eight people. Otherwise, the group might rely on the most knowledge-

able person for the answers, finish quickly, and learn very little.

7. Debrief the exercise. Have a spokesperson from each group report the group's answer to each question. So as not to duplicate discussion, ask other groups if they have a different answer or additional issues to bring up. Then repeat the process for the next question, and so on, until completion.

8. Summarize the discussion, highlighting key issues, and match theory and practice.

Circulars and Periodicals: Managing the Mail

M ost managers are inundated with periodicals, circulars, and fliers about training courses, products, and services.

- There are certain benefits in receiving this material:
  - ✓ Free information about training trends
  - ✓ Useful information about current organization issues and priorities
  - ✓ Up-to-date labor market information
  - ✓ Case studies
  - ✓ An overview of the options available (course lengths and costs), which facilitates decisions about course selection
  - ✓ Information about training aids, job aids, and multimedia training solutions
  - ✓ Up-to-date course and video catalogs
  - ✓ Topical reading lists
- On the other hand, it requires judgment and experience to decide what to keep and what to throw out.
- Your strategy for managing this mountain of paper will depend on your needs, time, and support staff. Nevertheless, there are some techniques for managing the mail:
  - ✓ Set up binders for important circulars, and put the circulars in the binders on receipt. You can read them at your convenience.
  - ✓ Use accordion files for miscellaneous brochures about courses. Put all fliers into sections by month (it's too onerous to divide them up by topics). Keep them for only six months; after that information is almost always out of date.
  - ✓ Put brochures directly into the accordion file, to review when you need to. Letting them collect on your desk is discouraging and distracting.
  - ✓ Schedule half a day each month to review material you've

received. Write a one-page summary of observations about trends, statistics, and labor market information you've noticed, and keep these summaries in a separate binder—your "food for thought" binder.

✓ Take half an hour each month to throw out material that has accumulated in your "stale-dated" categories.

✓ Explore your closest public library's business periodicals; then cancel any subscriptions that you can easily read at the library. The same applies to professional associations.

✓ If your organization maintains a library or archives, send all literature older than two months for safekeeping there. You've gained some space without losing access to the material.

✓ Keep a "pending" file for unsolicited proposals so that you can refer to them when consultants call to follow up. This is much more effective than making promises about calling back when you've received the material or suggesting that they call you "in two weeks."

✓ When scanning your mail, beware of offers for free issues of magazines or periodicals. You may find that you receive issues past the free offer, for which you will be billed.

✓ Quickly reroute information that is relevant to other departments. Keep preprinted routing slips on hand for this purpose.

✓ Don't be afraid to throw out brochures that have little or no relevance to your needs. Toss them as soon as you receive them.

✓ Use the information and advertisements that you receive as a handy source of inspiration when writing proposals or projects. These professional presentation pieces often contain excellent summaries on organization issues, training methodology, key learning principles, and related research findings.

Coaching

Coaching is a key skill for any manager. Coaching time will lead to improved performance if you follow these principles.

- Good coaches train people to do the job right every time. Although most coaching is done in technical areas of a job, you can also coach people to improve their team and interpersonal skills.
- Meet daily with people, either collectively or individually, to obtain agreement on what is expected of them.
- Use these methods to help employees reach their goals:
  - ✓ *Mentoring.* Model the skills you expect others to use.
  - ✓ *Counseling.* Help your associates find solutions through step-by-step self-discovery.
  - ✓ *Training.* Increase your associates' skills by explaining what you want them to do, showing them how to do it, letting them try while you observe, and giving them feedback on their performance.
  - ✓ *Confronting.* Let your associates know when their behavior fails to meet agreed-on standards.
- If associates fail to do the job right, show them again. Ask them to confirm their understanding of the task. Have them demonstrate their understanding by showing you how to do the task.
- If the task is large or appears difficult, break it into pieces. Learning one step at a time will build any trainee's self-confidence.
- If associates do not improve after a number of trials, determine whether the cause is attitudinal or a lack of aptitude. If it is the latter, move the person to a job that better suits his or her skill. If it is attitudinal, determine the cause and solution. If this does not work—and only a small minority will not respond—go through the disciplinary procedure, and terminate the individual.
- Give people regular feedback. Wherever possible, measure

their performance so that they know when they are improving or getting worse.

- As people's skills improve, encourage them to discover new and better ways of working. Praise them for their new ideas.
- Allow people to improvise, even if the new method does not fit your perception of the best method. Encourage a spirit of enterprise.
- Always:
  - ✓ Role-model what you expect of others.
  - ✓ Provide encouragement for people to do better.
  - ✓ Let people know when they have met or exceeded expectations. Tell them immediately, and specify what you observed. Ask them how they felt about the improvement and how they expect the improvement to continue.
  - ✓ Inform the employee who has not done well:
    - As soon as possible.
    - In a place out of sight of other employees.
    - By being specific about what you are dissatisfied with.
    - By finding out how the person feels.
    - By focusing on the problem, not the person. Always use "I" rather than "you" statements.
    - By never using foul language.
    - By involving the trainee in finding a solution.
    - By summarizing expectations clearly.
    - Assertively rather than in an apologetic manner.

Computer-Based Training

Computers are becoming a dominant tool for training, as well as the predominant tool for communicating. In fact, this medium is growing faster than other forms of training delivery. Here is an overview on the use of computer-based training (CBT).

- CBT refers to learning that is conducted using a computer. This includes interactive videodisk instruction, CD-ROM, the Internet, and computer software.
- CBT is a fascinating and exciting medium for training, but it is by no means immune to problems associated with poor design.
- As more people become exposed to animation and virtual reality and the sophistication of video games, it has become increasingly challenging to design CBT that will challenge, stimulate, and hold the attention of learners for any reasonable time, let alone teach them.
- Experience shows that CBT, like other forms of training, needs to be:
  - ✓ Specific to one topic.
  - ✓ Customized for a particular organization or industry.
  - ✓ Integrated into other forms of learning that will reinforce and lend variety to the learning experience.
- CBT can never take the place of human interaction.
- Viewing CBT as the ultimate and only form of training is unrealistic.
- CBT is most effective when it is designed to work like the human brain, an undisciplined organ that likes to flow from one idea to another. Hence CBT that provides only for multiple-choice responses or enables a person to move from one screen to the next in a predesigned sequence will be far less effective than a process that:

✓ Allows the learner to move to topics of his or her choice in a random fashion.

✓ Provides feedback on the learner's effectiveness, particularly when the person has made a mistake.

✓ Enables the learner to use a variety of tools to navigate through the learning process.

- CBT that relies on sound, animation, and color to maintain learners' attention is a lot less effective than a technology that allows for an interactive response through video clips or responsive animation.

Conducting a Training Session

The relationship between the trainer and participants is an important element in creating lasting change through training. There are many factors that contribute to setting up and maintaining a positive learning environment. Here's a handy checklist to review before any training session.

On the Day of the Session

- The better you prepare your material, the better you will be able to pay attention to important signals and adjust your style and lessons accordingly.
- Get to the training room early to give yourself time to set up and greet the early birds.
- Check the view from several seats to ensure that everyone can see the overhead screen and flip chart(s).
- Check all equipment. If you are using a slide or overhead projector, make sure that you know how it works and that it in fact does work. Have spare bulbs handy.
- Make sure you have coffee, tea, and juice available before the start. People shouldn't rely entirely on you to wake them up.
- Get comfortable with participants before the official start. Mingle with them to establish rapport.
- Determine before you start if some members of the group are waiting for phone calls. This gives you a better sense of who *needs* to leave the room versus those who *want* to leave the room.

At the Start of the Session

- Begin on a high note. Memorize the opening to start off strongly and set the tone for the workshop, or get a senior manager to open the workshop. Enlisting a superior adds credibility to the session by stressing the commitment of the top.

- At the onset, tell the participants what you expect of them and what they can expect of you. Remind them that:
  - ✓ They are responsible for their own learning.
  - ✓ They should let you know if their needs are not being met.
  - ✓ You will be starting and finishing on time.
- Provide other important information—for example:
  - ✓ Fire exit location
  - ✓ Telephone availability
  - ✓ Rest room locations
- Introduce yourself, and get people to introduce themselves or have them interview one another.
- Make the objectives of the program clear. Post them where they can be clearly seen.
- Review the agenda, and relate it to the objectives.
- Acknowledge that people have varying degrees of enthusiasm about training. You will thus demonstrate respect to your listeners and pragmatism.

During Training

- Keep on schedule. You can do this if you:
  - ✓ Negotiate break lengths with participants.
  - ✓ Note restarting times on the flip chart.
  - ✓ Don't wait for stragglers. Close the door at the agreed-on starting time.
  - ✓ Don't summarize for people who come in late.
- If the session doesn't go according to plan, don't raise awareness of the problem by apologizing unless the snafu is obvious.
- You will enhance learning if you:
  - ✓ Create an active environment by encouraging participation.
  - ✓ Deal with one subject at a time.
  - ✓ Move from the simple to the complex.
  - ✓ Start from the known and then progress to the new.
  - ✓ Have participants use as many of their five senses as possible.

✓ Encourage the use of visualization.

✓ Review one segment of training before moving on to the next.

- Don't be afraid to admit you don't have an answer to a question. Ask the others if they have the answer. If not, offer to get back to the person. Don't lie or wing it. Your integrity and honesty could be compromised and, with it, your ability to influence the audience.

- Avoid using jargon and complex words like *parameter* or *virtual*. Such words indicate that you are being theoretical and not down to earth.

- Use visuals wherever possible. They are six to eight times more effective than verbal instructions. You can use drawings, diagrams, and flowcharts.

- Make sure that diagrams and drawings are culturally neutral. For example, a skull and bones means danger or poison in Western culture but represents the spiritual soul in others.

- Stop from time to time to poll the audience. Ask, for example, "How many of you have tried this?" A poll provides a welcome change of pace and gives you useful information.

- Repeat or rephrase questions if you think that not everyone in the audience heard.

- Vary the pace and presentation techniques to keep interest high. Remember that the attention span of most adults is about seven minutes, so change the tempo and presentation medium, and intersperse team tasks with individual assignments.

- Draw information out of the group wherever possible. Audience participation provides a change of pace and also validates your ideas in practical terms.

- Pay attention to the audience's body language; rolled eyes and crossed arms, for example, may indicate resistance.

- Observe the amount of note taking going on, a good indicator of individual involvement.

- Don't automatically interpret a lack of responsiveness as resistance. Some people are naturally reticent, or they may be embarrassed about their language skills (accents, stuttering, etc.).

- Walk around during breakout sessions, and join each group for a short time, noting the interaction and involvement of each participant.

- Make sure that some of the breakout sessions are for pairs. This gives you a clearer picture of individual involvement as you walk around.
- Don't stay rooted to one spot. Moving about facilitates one-on-one eye contact and good clues about participants' energy levels and attitudes.
- Always be alert for clues (rolled eyes, bowed heads, scribbling, etc.) that the group wants you to "shut down" long-winded participants.
- Ask for volunteers on at least two or three occasions. Enthusiasm (or lack of it) is a good barometer of group involvement.
- Energy levels are lowest after lunch. Try to keep lunch light, to avoid afternoon drowsiness.

At the End of the Session

- End with a challenge. Ask everyone to commit to using some part of the workshop lesson in the next two weeks. Ask each person how he or she intends to do so.
- Ask people to write their action plans on a sheet of paper. Put these into self-addressed envelopes, and mail them to participants sixty days after the workshop.

Conferences and Seminars

C ompanies deal daily with a wealth of literature that advertises professional development opportunities and requests from staff to attend.

- These venues include:
  - ✓ Industry events.
  - ✓ Exhibitor events.
  - ✓ Professional association conferences.
  - ✓ Annual conventions.
  - ✓ Special-interest networking forums.
  - ✓ Executive development courses.
  - ✓ External seminars for developing business skills.
- Common issues for all companies concerning these venues are:
  - ✓ Costs to attend.
  - ✓ Selection of candidates.
  - ✓ Benefits to the company.
- Here are some guidelines for managing corporate funds and expectations for these forums:
  - ✓ Set annual budgets based on historical information and research about upcoming events.
  - ✓ Set corporate guidelines for attendance that emphasize business-based courses.
  - ✓ Identify courses that complement corporate succession planning processes, and prioritize candidates accordingly.
  - ✓ Request names of past participants from conference organizers, and do reference checking to help determine anticipated results from the session.
  - ✓ Take advantage of free presentations as often as is practical as sources of up-to-date information.
  - ✓ Beware of events that are actually organized sales pitches (especially when there is a fee).
  - ✓ Many conferences offer free tickets in exchange for services

(e.g., working the registration table or supplying a speaker from your company).

✓ Most conferences offer partial tickets for key events.

✓ Ensure that a list of participants and a summary of speakers' materials is included in the registration fee.

✓ Require your company's attendee to prepare a synopsis of key information from the conference. Make course materials available for circulation and reference for other employees.

✓ Do follow-up networking with other participants to maximize your investment.

✓ Conduct ongoing research with other companies to help set cost and attendance guidelines.

✓ Equip your company representatives with information kits about your products or services for networking.

✓ Coach your company representatives about their role as ambassadors for your company at these events.

Consultants

Caveat emptor.

For every consulting success story, there's a story about poor service, outrageous prices, and dashed expectations. The availability of consulting firms and independent entrepreneurs presents greater choices than ever before. At the same time, checking credibility can be a challenge, yet no organization can afford poor service.

- Consultants provide a number of advantages:
  - ✓ Up-to-date training expertise in specialized areas
  - ✓ Lower-cost solutions for repeated training needs or one-time-only initiatives
  - ✓ A fresh perspective for employees
  - ✓ Labor market information gained from working with a number of companies or industries
  - ✓ Responsiveness, to meet tight deadlines
  - ✓ Skills and programs that are not available in-house
- Some disadvantages in dealing with consultants are that they:
  - ✓ Have less commitment to an organization's long-term success.
  - ✓ Cost more, on an hourly basis, than internal training staff.
  - ✓ Work for your competitors too and may jeopardize confidentiality.
  - ✓ May not have an in-depth appreciation of your organization's culture.
  - ✓ Will want to be paid no matter how successful (or unsuccessful) the initiative is.
- Managers are bombarded with calls from consultants offering their services. Here are some suggestions for managing a high volume of unsolicited calls:

- ✓ *Never* be rude. You represent your organization at all times, and any bad manners on your part reflects on your company.
- ✓ Request literature from consultants before agreeing to a meeting. This material will give you a sense of the professionalism of the consultant and client references.
- ✓ Designate one afternoon a month to meet with prospective consultants.
- ✓ Mail out copies of your organization's training catalog to callers. This will save time on both sides so that consultants won't pitch for programs that you already have.
- ✓ Prepare a semiannual summary of your training needs to send to callers so that you will hear back only from those who are able to meet your requirements.
- ✓ Designate a junior training employee to meet with callers to screen those who may meet your needs.
- ✓ Ask callers about their industry expertise, client references, and training credentials.
- ✓ Ask callers about their perspective on training trends and organization challenges to gain a sense of their experience.
- ✓ Meet with some consultants from time to time. They bring information about the marketplace.
- ✓ Keep all literature you receive from consultants during the year. This is an excellent source of competitive information and research.
- Before hiring a consultant, make the following determinations:
  - ✓ How good is their reputation? You don't judge a book by the cover, so don't base your evaluation on the slickness of their brochures or the performance of their presentation.
  - ✓ How did they contact you? Was it a reference or a cold call?
  - ✓ What makes the consultant uniquely qualified to help you with the particular challenge you have?
  - ✓ How credible are the consultant's references?
  - ✓ How similar have the consultant's other assignments been to your own, and how effective has the training been?
- During an interview meeting with a consultant, establish:
  - ✓ What makes their organization special. What innovative work has it done?
  - ✓ Whether the consultant is using your organization as a test site for a new program.

✓ What written materials will be made available to the trainees. Will they be customized?

✓ How flexible they are around specific issues you have about
costs, numbers of trainees, and the time of training (eve-
nings, weekends, etc.).

✓ Whether the consultant will provide you with a written
outline of the program, including course objectives.

✓ How the effectiveness of the training will be measured.

✓ If any guarantees about improvement are given in measurable formats.

✓ The professional qualifications and experience of the
trainer who will be working on your assignment.

✓ The personality and motivational style of the trainer. Given
the culture of your organization, will that style fit?

✓ How flexible the trainer is in terms of course duration and
course content. (Short, punchy modules over a period of
time are more effective than lengthy three-day workshops).

✓ Whether your staff will have a direct hot line to the trainer
whenever they need support or advice.

✓ What homework the consultant has done about your organization in terms of size, market niche, competitive edge,
and product lines.

✓ How competitive the fee structure is compared to others in
the field.

✓ Whether the quoted prices are inclusive, or whether there
are additional costs for duplication of materials, travel, and
other items.

✓ If and how often the consultant speaks at high-profile conferences.

✓ Whether the consultant has published articles in respected
journals or newspapers.

✓ Whether the consultant does work for any government?
(Governments are very strict in qualifying consultants.)

✓ If the trainer has backup in the event of sickness or other
emergency for a scheduled training course date.

✓ If the consultant belongs to any recognized professional associations.

✓ How long the consultant or consulting organization has
been in business.

✓ If the consultant has relevant experience in your industry.

- Despite your best efforts, there may be occasions that leave you feeling that your money was spent poorly and time was wasted. Examples of poor investments include:
  ✓ The majority of trainees considered the training a waste of time.
  ✓ You paid a premium price for a poor product.
  ✓ The consultant's conduct was unprofessional and resulted in complaints.
  ✓ Promised workbooks and videos for the session were not available.
- Here are some follow-up techniques that can minimize the impact of costly consulting mistakes:
  ✓ Negotiate for a reduced fee for the work already done.
  ✓ Negotiate for reduced fees for upcoming initiatives.
  ✓ Ask the consultant to prepare a recovery strategy at no extra cost.
  ✓ Ask the consultant to stage a free "lunch-and-learn" seminar.
  ✓ Review trainee evaluations with the consultant as a mutual learning opportunity.
  ✓ Apologize to trainees for any inappropriate or insensitive remarks the consultant made. Make it clear that this is not the company way!
  ✓ If you generally like the services of the consulting firm and are disappointed with one specific representative, ask for a replacement for the rest of the project.
  ✓ Explain your follow-up strategies to disappointed trainees.
  ✓ Do research and trainee follow-up to determine whether you are reacting to the opinions expressed by only a few malcontents.
  ✓ For long-term projects, pay a penalty fee to discontinue the initiative rather than hoping for the best if initial reviews are poor.
  ✓ Use every poor consulting experience as an opportunity to understand your role in setting realistic expectations.
- Consultants have rights too. It is difficult for them to be successful when companies don't deliver the information or access to background material that was promised. Changing delivery dates, cancelling meetings, or delaying payments is unprofessional—and it is behavior that you would never tolerate in a consultant.

Core Competencies

C ore competencies refer to performance dimensions, key success criteria, and success formulas. The belief behind them is that certain skills, traits, and attitudes will predispose individuals and companies to success. Therefore, identifying them and focusing on them in training will add value to the organization and help it meet its goals.

- Core competencies differ by company and industry. Nevertheless, in all cases, they reflect job content and success in terms of skills, knowledge, and personal characteristics.
- When defined, core competencies are integrated into the following organization practices:
  ✓ Organization design and restructuring
  ✓ Job evaluation systems
  ✓ Compensation strategy
  ✓ Performance measurement criteria and evaluation tools
  ✓ Recruitment planning
  ✓ Hiring criteria
  ✓ Training and development planning
  ✓ Promotion processes and succession planning
  ✓ Career planning.
  ✓ Performance evaluation
  ✓ Productivity analysis
- Core competency profiles for job content and employee success reflect a combination of both "hard" competencies and "soft" competencies.
- Common "hard" competencies for an organization include:
  ✓ Personnel management.
  ✓ Financial expertise.
  ✓ Business plan development and execution.
  ✓ Marketing expertise.
  ✓ Internal and external communications.
  ✓ Policy development and deployment.
  ✓ Sales skills.

- ✓ Customer relation skills.
- ✓ Project management.
- Common "soft" competencies for an organization include:
  - ✓ Directing work through others.
  - ✓ Developing others.
  - ✓ Influence skills.
  - ✓ Energy and enthusiasm.
  - ✓ Working with others.
  - ✓ Organization awareness.
  - ✓ Analysis and judgment.
  - ✓ Adaptability.
  - ✓ Change management.
  - ✓ Self-confidence.
  - ✓ Listening and responding.
  - ✓ Perseverance.
  - ✓ Consistency.
- Training and development professionals and line managers will be working more closely together than ever before in organizations that have developed core competencies. Together, they are refining training course content and selecting participants so that core competencies can be established.

Cost Controls

A training course that has high-priority impact shouldn't be abandoned because of an apparent high cost.

- Here are some measures that can reduce total costs so that key training interventions aren't shelved:
  - ✓ Train key participants, and use them as coaches for others.
  - ✓ Break down course material into modules to reduce the strain on daily operations.
  - ✓ Reduce lengthy courses to key teaching points, and supplement them with videos and books.
  - ✓ Set up partnerships with other companies to share the costs of common training courses.
  - ✓ Seek out government grants or industry association support for costs.
  - ✓ Split the costs of training with participants for personal development courses.
  - ✓ Negotiate with consultants for approval to reproduce training manuals in-house.
  - ✓ Negotiate volume discounts with consultants.
  - ✓ Conduct training after hours or on weekends.
  - ✓ Apply penalties to no-show scheduled trainees where costs are incurred to run the program.
  - ✓ Use in-house subject matter experts as facilitators.
  - ✓ Share costs with unions or other employee associations.
  - ✓ Explore lower-cost training provided through local colleges and universities.
  - ✓ Conduct training on site rather than at expensive hotels or conference facilities.
  - ✓ Trade training sites with local companies.
  - ✓ Set up volume discounts with airlines and hotels to reduce travel expenses.
  - ✓ Arrange lower consultant costs in exchange for free publicity.
  - ✓ Co-venture a new training program with a vendor. You get unlimited access; the vendor gets the copyright.

✓ Put together a group of organizations with similar needs for volume discounts or to fund all-new design.

- Travel costs for trainees and facilitators can be significant. They can even lead to delays or cancellation of important training projects. Here are some tips for reducing these costs:

  ✓ Videotape important sessions so that employees who cannot attend scheduled courses can understand the key teaching points. This is more cost-effective than makeup sessions.

  ✓ Set realistic limits for meals and incidental expenses during travel.

  ✓ Start training courses at noon so that out-of-town employees can save the cost of a hotel room the night before the session.

  ✓ For some training courses, videoconferencing can be a cost-effective alternative. If your company does not have its own facilities, explore the possibility of renting facilities at a local college or university.

  ✓ Provide incentives (dinner coupons, theater tickets, etc.) for employees to stay with friends or relatives during training at an out-of-town location.

Costs and Benefits of Training

Most companies would like to be able to measure the costs invested in training initiatives against anticipated results. The challenge is that it is far easier to measure the costs of conducting training than it is to quantify results. A useful tool in determining costs and savings is to compare costs per participant versus savings per participant.

Training Costs

- Training costs include:
  - ✓ Facilitator fees.
  - ✓ Training design.
  - ✓ Course materials.
  - ✓ Videos and workbooks.
  - ✓ Facilities rental.
  - ✓ Equipment rentals (overhead projectors, etc.).
  - ✓ Production downtime (including employee time off the job).
  - ✓ Videoconferencing facilities.
  - ✓ Specialized computer equipment.
  - ✓ Administration (registration procedures, confirmation notices, etc.).
- All of the relevant costs, divided by the anticipated number of participants, gives the cost per participant.

Savings Generated by Training

- Savings generated by training initiatives include:
  - ✓ Error rate reductions.
  - ✓ Reduced customer turnover.

✓ Reduced equipment downtime.
✓ Increased revenue collection.
✓ Accelerated equipment start-up time.
✓ Reduced employee turnover, when turnover is attributable to poor supervision.
✓ Proper implementation of new customer strategies.
✓ Higher workplace morale through more effective management practices.
✓ Less time lost to grievance hearings and work stoppages because of ineffective supervision.
✓ Reduced recruitment costs (because training can create more job-ready candidates for promotions).
✓ Maximized productivity of new employees through efficient orientation training.

Calculating Potential Savings

- To calculate potential savings, it is imperative to set goals for posttraining achievements by identifying and quantifying the changes a training initiative will produce. The relevant factors in the formula are

  ✓ Current level of performance (e.g., 200 error rates per month; 6 lost customer accounts per month; 5 days lost to work stoppages per year).
  ✓ Translate the current level of performance into a dollar figure—for example:

  $$200 \text{ error rates} \times 5 \text{ minutes correction time}$$
  $$\times \$15 \text{ salary per hour}$$
  $$= \$250 \text{ per month.}$$

  ✓ Identify the change that training can produce (e.g., reduce errors to 50 per month).
  ✓ Calculate the savings that the target criteria will generate—for example:

  $$200 \text{ errors} - 50 \text{ errors}$$
  $$= \text{decrease of 150 errors per month}$$
  $$\text{savings} = 150 \times 5 \text{ minutes}/60 \times \$15 =$$
  $$\$187.50.$$

✓ Identify a meaningful time line for realizing savings, based on your best business predictions about factors contributing to errors remaining unchanged.
✓ Identify the number of employees in the target training group.
- Divide the total anticipated savings by the number of participants to identify the savings per participant.

Comparing Costs to Savings

1. Multiply the cost per participant by the total number of participants.
2. Multiply the savings per participant by the total number of participants.
3. Compare your figures to establish your business case for training.

This exercise not only identifies actual costs and realistic savings but will also ensure that your training expectations are reasonable and targeted to measurable business outcomes.

Development Plans for Employees: Criteria for Success

From time to time, people will be singled out as potential leaders in the organization. These employees can be developed in many ways, including taking responsibility for a special project.

- A new assignment, given to challenge and develop an employee, will be more successful if the trainee:
  - ✓ Knows that both success and failure are possible, and this will be obvious to those following the progress of the task. With the belief that there is a fair chance of success, the right person will be motivated to overcome all obstacles.
  - ✓ Needs to use initiative to get things done. Needing to show leadership and taking charge will motivate the individual to develop a clear vision of what he or she is aiming to do and develop skills.
  - ✓ Is required to work with a variety of people.
  - ✓ Is required to work under pressure caused by factors such as needing to meet tough deadlines, travel extensively, or work long hours.
  - ✓ Is involved in a strategically important task.
  - ✓ Is required to initiate or recommend actions that will have widespread organization ramifications, such as restructuring, downsizing, or reengineering.
  - ✓ Needs to influence people over whom the person has no direct control (e.g., people outside the organization, peers in other work areas, and people higher in the corporate structure).
  - ✓ Does not have a fixed route to achieve the objectives set out. This will necessitate that the person make decisions or solve problems.

✓ Is monitored by key people inside and outside the organization.
✓ Needs to develop a new team or improve the performance of an existing group.
✓ Is intellectually challenged and deals with ambiguity (e.g., having to challenge existing policies).
✓ Has significant roadblocks to overcome, such as lack of top management support or insufficient resources.

Difficult Behavior During Training

I t is said that trainers have to deal with three types of people:

1. *Learners*, who want to be there and get as much as they can from the session.
2. *Vacationers*, who want to have as much fun and free time as possible.
3. *Prisoners*, who resent being there.

A training session can be thrown off course by a variety of unco-operative behavior. Here are the most frequent types and the ideas to deal with each.

The Negative Person

- Most often the frustration is legitimate. Your goal is to help the participant to find a good reason for being at the training session.
- Allow the person to vent and get any frustrations off his or her chest. Then you can decide whether to:
  - ✓ Empathize and ask if you can move on.
  - ✓ Empathize and determine if the issue needs to be dealt with right away.
  - ✓ Empathize and offer to deal with the issue later or at the end of the meeting.
- Control your response:
  - ✓ Don't take the issue personally.
  - ✓ Don't get drawn into an argument.
  - ✓ Don't show anger. Keep calm (outwardly), and keep a straight face. If you show that the negative person is getting to you, you will be demonstrating publicly a lack of ability to deal with the situation.
- If the person is making wild, exaggerated statements, canvass

other opinions. This way the person will be made to understand that his or her opinions do not represent those held by others in the workshop.

- Ask the frustrated learner to give you ideas as to how to deal with the difficulties.
- Call a time-out and regroup. Collect your thoughts and composure. Take the time to revise your strategy to deal with the problem.
- Let peer pressure deal with the culprit.
- Address antagonistic questions as serious and legitimate. Simply answer them and move on.

The Overly Talkative Participant

- Establish a learning contract at the beginning of the session that includes the concept of giving everyone an equal opportunity to participate. If there are continuing interruptions, remind the person diplomatically of the contract and the importance of getting other perspectives.
- Jump in when the person stops to catch his or her breath, and echo the person's comments. For example, say, "So what I'm hearing is that . . . Thank you. Now who else has something to add that has not already been covered?"
- Do a round robin to ensure equal opportunity to use the available time. Say, "Let's go around the table and get one idea from each person. If you don't have an idea, just say *Pass*."
- Frequent eye contact with the person will serve to invite additional comment. Avoid it.
- Direct questions to people other than the talkative person.
- Talk to the person privately at a break, and stress the importance of letting everyone have a chance to respond.

The Rambler

- Summarize the person's ideas in order to bring clarity before moving on.
- Emphasize the importance of staying on schedule.

- Record the ideas offered on a flip chart. This will reduce repetition and force the person to organize his or her thoughts.

General Preparation Strategies

- Your best strategy for anticipated difficulties during training is getting good information beforehand about the group and its dynamics:
  - ✓ Review the evaluations from other groups to whom you've given the course. Pay particular attention to which topics generated the least interest or most confusion, and analyze why.
  - ✓ Talk with the manager or managers of the participants. Find out as much as you can about learning styles, communication styles, and general enthusiasm about training.
  - ✓ Get a sense about other organization issues that may be playing on the trainees' minds—for example, downsizing, new performance measures, or upcoming management changes.
  - ✓ Develop a demographic profile of the group to see whether there is some natural tension among participants already (e.g., managers attending along with their direct reports).
  - ✓ Conduct an informal telephone survey with some participants to understand their expectations and previous positive and negative training experiences.
  - ✓ Talk to someone who has trained the group before. What are this person's observations?

Diversity in the Classroom

W orkplace demographics can create challenges for trainers, especially those who believe that trainees share their perspectives, values, and backgrounds. Insensitivity will compromise trainers' professionalism and learning outcomes too.

- Diversity encompasses these areas:
  - ✓ Ethnic diversity
  - ✓ Cultural diversity
  - ✓ Gender ratios
  - ✓ Age distribution
  - ✓ Physical capabilities
  - ✓ Experience in the workplace
- Diversity in the classroom reflects the diversity in the customer base. Learning to understand and appreciate different perceptions about service and value has become a hallmark of successful companies.

Here are some guidelines for ensuring that your demeanor, lessons, and exercises communicate respect for all participants.

- Start sessions by encouraging everyone to participate in a brief introduction. This will give you a good sense of the communication styles, language fluency, and ease of the participants.
- During your introduction, ask participants to speak about their overall work experience. This is not only informative but also shows respect for all prior work experience.
- At the beginning of the session, offer to spend break time helping anyone who has difficulty with the lessons. This avoids embarrassing trainees who might feel belittled in dealing at greater length with an issue that they feel is easy or trivial for others yet difficult or important to them.
- Check beforehand whether there are special equipment or access requirements for some trainees.

- Avoid using examples or anecdotes that may not be meaningful to everyone (e.g., old TV programs or local history events).
- Don't use sexist language, such as referring to managers as "he" and secretaries as "she."
- Change the composition of breakout teams regularly throughout the day to help participants hear many different points of view.
- If a trainee is lip-reading, always face him or her and speak clearly and slowly.
- Don't automatically speak louder or more slowly to someone with an accent. The person's hearing and comprehension may be just fine, and you run the risk of appearing condescending.
- Watch out for unwitting references to your own culture (e.g., "going to church," "the Protestant work ethic," or "we all grew up knowing that").
- *Never* make a sexist or racist remark or joke, even if the group appears homogeneous. You can never be sure of individual backgrounds and sensitivities. More important, these comments are *always* inappropriate.
- Never acknowledge a racist or sexist remark from participants. Just ignore it. If someone persists, speak to the person privately at the first break.
- Monitor the group carefully to understand who is having difficulty understanding the lessons because of language barriers. Adjust your style accordingly.
- Be knowledgeable about religious holidays for all major groups, and avoid scheduling training on those days.
- Take religious dietary prohibitions and restrictions into account when arranging luncheon menus.
- Choose videos that reflect current workforce demographics.
- Respect participants' personal space. Not everyone is comfortable with a tap on the shoulder, an arm around the shoulder, or a group hug.
- Beware of physical exercises that may challenge or embarrass some participants.
- Be sensitive to the fact that there are hidden differences that people may not be willing to disclose (e.g., sexual preference, disabilities, health conditions). Be sure the content and your comments respect these differences.

Evaluating Training

There are three reasons for evaluating a training program's effectiveness:

1. To identify areas of improvement
2. To determine whether a course should be continued or canceled
3. To assess a program's role in an integrated training strategy

There are four sequential levels in an evaluation process:

Level One, Reaction. Trainees' verbal and written feedback at the end of a course

Level Two, Learning. Trainee's understanding of the key learning principles.

Level Three, Behavior. Observable application of the skill on the job.

Level Four, Results. Quantifiable improvements in productivity that can be attributed to the training.

Here are some techniques for gathering useful information for all four levels of evaluation.

Level One: Reaction to the Training

- Design a user-friendly reaction form that participants complete at the end of a training course. Leave room on it for comments and suggestions.
- Have participants rate and comment on the conditions of training, as well as the content (e.g., facilities, length of course, course materials).
- Balance the questions between course content and course delivery (facilitation, materials, etc.).

- To ensure that all participants complete the form, set aside time on the agenda for this. It is extremely difficult to collect forms even twenty-four hours after the course.
- If the organization's culture values openness, encourage participants to put their name on the form.
- Change the order of questions on evaluation forms from course to course, and customize the content. Participants will consider their responses more carefully.
- Do some informal follow-up one to two weeks after the course. Ask participants if they have changed their mind about the evaluation they submitted.

Level Two: Understanding

- Determine whether the course was intended to change:
  - ✓ Attitudes.
  - ✓ Skills.
  - ✓ Knowledge.
  - ✓ A combination of these factors.
- Use preseminar tests or quizzes to gauge the level of skills, knowledge, or attitudes before the training.
- Design a postcourse test to determine new levels of skills, knowledge, or attitudes. Have participants complete the test two to three months after the training.
- Ensure that participants view this testing as a tool for evaluating the training, *not* the trainee.
- Apply the same postcourse test to employees who did not attend the course but are responsible for similar results. Compare the results to the trainees' results.
- Create simulation exercises for trainees to apply newly learned techniques.
- Use a skill checklist to evaluate participants on a given skill.

Level Three: Behavior Change

- This phase assesses the likelihood that trainees will apply new skills, knowledge, or attitudes back on the job. This level of evaluation typically occurs about six months after training.

- Use 360° feedback to document observable changes.
- Use productivity reports or other data that relate directly to new skills to assess precourse and postcourse competence.
- Determine what kinds of incentives are in place to encourage the practice of newly learned techniques. If there are none, work with management to create conditions that encourage success.
- Determine what barriers might exist to practicing new techniques. Work with the management team to minimize or remove barriers before evaluating results.
- Consider what tools, resources, or equipment trainees need to use their new skills and evaluate changed behavior where optional conditions for success are in place.

Level Four: Achieving Quantifiable Results

- Results are quantifiable outcomes that were identified in the up-front analysis.
- The key question for this level of evaluation is: Has a problem been solved or a gap been closed?
- Following are examples of changes that you're looking for:
  - ✓ Fewer errors
  - ✓ Increased customer satisfaction
  - ✓ Reduced infractions of policies or standards
  - ✓ Faster production time
- This phase of the evaluation process is similar to a cost-benefit analysis. Results are assessed in the context of the time and money invested in the training program and the length of time required to achieve the desired results.
- The time frame for measuring results after training is directly related to the size or extent of the problem or opportunity that the training addressed. The greater the changes required are, the longer the evaluation period is.
- As a general rule, results should be evaluated at least three months after training and by not later than twelve months. After twelve months, the conditions for success have usually changed significantly, and it becomes more difficult to measure results directly related to specific training initiatives.

Evaluation Forms: Design and Use

As training budgets shrink and training needs escalate, most organizations are taking a longer-term view to measuring training results. Nevertheless, postcourse evaluation forms remain an important resource in the overall evaluation process.

- The postcourse evaluation is a customer satisfaction tool that should measure these course elements:
  ✓ Meeting trainees' expectations
  ✓ Timeliness of the course
  ✓ Length of the course
  ✓ Organization and flow of lessons and materials
  ✓ Facilitation effectiveness
  ✓ Immediate learning outcomes
  ✓ Facility, location, and comfort of the room
  ✓ Quality of materials (binders, handouts, videos, etc.)
  ✓ Pacing
  ✓ Relevance of the lesson to the job
  ✓ Relevance of the lesson to long-term professional development
  ✓ Suggestions about training material
  ✓ Suggestions about facilitator style
  ✓ Most relevant and least relevant lessons
  ✓ Food and accommodations

Here are some suggestions that can help you to develop a meaningful postcourse evaluation form.

- Customize a standard form to take into account specific objectives and conditions for the training. The more relevant the form is, the more likely it will be completed.
- Use a satisfaction scale of 1 to 6 instead of 1 to 5. This scale provides more meaningful gradations and avoids the widespread tendency to assign a 3 rating (which tells you little).

- Use a mixture of open and closed questions—for example, "Would you recommend the course to others?" "Why or why not?" "List three things you have learned."
- Ask for overall ratings for both the course and the facilitator.
- Ask for comments about the level of participation.
- Balance questions that have positive and negative biases (e.g., "most relevant/least relevant")
- Include time for completing evaluations in the course schedule.
- Solicit suggestions about ideal resources and conditions for implementing key learning principles.
- Use time frames to help you assess the application of the learning principles ("I expect to use my new skills: (a) immediately, (b) in three months, (c) in six months").
- Commit to sending a summary of the evaluations to all participants. This will underscore the importance you place on their feedback.
- Names and other identifying information should be optional.
- Ask for suggestions about designing an even more useful evaluation form. Most people enjoy the opportunity to be creative and are pleased when their ideas are sought.
- If the course is several days in length, do a brief evaluation at the end of the first day to see if you are on track.
- The postcourse evaluation form should be easy to read, easy to answer, and provide information that prepares you for more in-depth and long-term course effectiveness indicators. A sample is provided in Exhibit 3.

Exhibit 3. Sample evaluation sheet.

I value your feedback. Please respond candidly to the following questions and rate the workshop on each criterion listed below:

Seminar Content	Exceeded Expec- tations	Met Expec- tations	Needs Improve- ment	Not Appli- cable
Material organization	❏	❏	❏	❏
Presentation level	❏	❏	❏	❏
Practicality of material to my job	❏	❏	❏	❏
Quality of written materials	❏	❏	❏	❏
Small group activities	❏	❏	❏	❏
Visual aids	❏	❏	❏	❏
Presentation				
Presentation style	❏	❏	❏	❏
Speaker's knowledge of subject	❏	❏	❏	❏
Coverage of material clear	❏	❏	❏	❏
Response to questions	❏	❏	❏	❏

SUGGESTIONS FOR IMPROVEMENT:

_____

_____

OTHER COMMENTS:

_____

_____

Please check the rating that best reflects your overall evaluation of this session.

EXCELLENT	GOOD	FAIR	POOR
❏	❏	❏	❏

Facilitator Tips: The Top Ten

Most trainees help the facilitator to succeed. Here's some advice from the pros that will help any facilitator get the group on his or her side.

1. Shake hands with participants as they enter the room to establish a one-on-one relationship.
2. Substitute the word *and* for the word *but* whenever possible. For example: "You've made an interesting point, and your colleagues disagree with you." You've lost nothing in your message, yet have reduced the risk of alienating the trainee.
3. Lean into the group when the discussion gets heated. It's a sign of respect, if not necessarily agreement.
4. Ask for suggestions from the group in answering difficult questions.
5. Nod your head as you listen to suggestions, to emphasize acute listening and interest.
6. Walk around the room as much as possible, so that you are close to people when engaging them in discussion.
7. Monitor the group carefully to gauge energy levels. Call for breaks when you sense lagging attention.
8. Use participants' names as often as possible.
9. Make it clear through examples and language that you respect the intelligence of the group members.
10. Establish at the start what kinds of discussions and issues are unrelated and inappropriate for this session. Examples would be: salaries and benefits; personality issues.

Facilitator Turnoffs: The Top Ten

H ere are some don'ts from real pros about facilitator behavior: trainees themselves.

1. Exaggerated or insincere enthusiasm about delivering the training.
2. Too many personal anecdotes that are irrelevant to the topic at hand.
3. Inadequate preparation.
4. Delaying the start of training to accommodate latecomers.
5. Staying rooted to one spot.
6. Not managing participants who monopolize conversation.
7. Talking down to the group.
8. Conducting childish games.
9. Reading verbatim from overheads rather than expanding on key points.
10. Not finishing the training on time.

Facilities: How to Choose Them

C lassroom training can be conducted on or away from company premises. Here are some guidelines to help you find the best venue.

- Following is a checklist of items that all good sites have:
  - ✓ Nearby rest rooms
  - ✓ A telephone number for messages for participants
  - ✓ Message board
  - ✓ Nearby breakout rooms
  - ✓ Adequate coat racks
  - ✓ Access to good equipment (flip charts, markers, wall space to put flip charts, etc.)
  - ✓ Lighting controls
  - ✓ Electrical outlets placed conveniently for equipment usage
  - ✓ Coffee service table
  - ✓ Trash containers
  - ✓ Comfortable chairs and tables
  - ✓ Public transportation access
  - ✓ Adequate parking
  - ✓ Handicap access
  - ✓ Transportation arrangements to and from local airports
  - ✓ Early morning access
  - ✓ Close to a variety of good eating places

Costs

- Costs vary depending on your needs, but be sure a contract addresses these costs:
  - ✓ The room
  - ✓ Equipment rental
  - ✓ Coffee and lunch service
  - ✓ Breakout rooms

✓ Cancellation penalty
✓ Discounts for trainees who are staying overnight in the fa-
  cility
✓ Volume discounts for frequent use

Facilities

- Using hotels for off-site training can be expensive. Here are
  some lower-cost alternatives:
  ✓ Company boardrooms and conference rooms
  ✓ Local educational institutions
  ✓ Boards of trade facilities
  ✓ Training vendor facilities
  ✓ Training rooms in other companies
  ✓ Government facilities (e.g., city hall)
  ✓ Industry association facilities
  ✓ Professional association facilities
  ✓ Public libraries
- Urge your staff to be creative in suggesting training sites. One
  enterprising company held seminars in different employee
  homes for seminars with fewer than twenty people. The donor
  received a floral arrangement and all food left over from the
  luncheon buffet. The trainees enjoyed a comfortable learning
  environment while enjoying a team member's hospitality.

Failure of Training: Reasons

Training can fail to satisfy the needs of the customer for a variety of reasons.

- *The reason for training has not been identified.*

  Solution: Identify performance gaps and find root causes. Training should be provided only if the major problem is a lack of training.

- *Training dollars are spread around to provide some training for everyone.*

  Solution: Adopt the 80/20 rule: allocate 80 percent of your resources to 20 percent of your people and 20 percent of your programs.

- *The training tries to be all things to all people.*

  Solution: Examine the key business strategies your organization is adopting to succeed. Provide most of your resources to help this initiative directly or indirectly.

- *Measures of effectiveness have nothing to do with the needs of the client but relate instead to the goals of the training department (e.g., numbers trained, number of programs offered, reaction of trainees at the end of the session).*

  Solution: Measure the effectiveness of the training in terms of changes of behavior, improvements in performance, or increases in customer satisfaction.

- ✓ *The needs of the trainees were ignored or not taken into account.*

  Solution: Conduct a needs analysis prior to the workshop to find out participants' knowledge of the topic, previous training, their key objectives, their attitude toward the topic, and any roadblocks that might prevent them from using the skills you will be teaching.

- ✓ *The training is impractical.*

  Solution: In meeting with the subject matter experts before the training, get real case studies so that you can match theory with practice. Also, ensure that you do not overburden the learners with theory; rather, spend most of your time discussing how they will use the training in the workplace.

✓ *Examples are unrealistic or unrelated.*

Solution: Find examples from the learners' own industry or type of work. Use examples of how ordinary people have applied the principles, rather than drawing on examples of industry titans.

✓ *The training is concentrated.*

Solution: Divide the training into modules that can be spread over time. Participants will have the opportunity to go back to work and put into practice the skills that they learned, then return to share their experiences and learn further skills.

✓ *The supervisor is not involved.*

Solution: Meet with the manager before the session and explain the program and its objective to him or her. Have him or her introduce the session, demonstrating organization support. Provide feedback to the supervisor at the end of the session, asking this person to follow up and promote the use of the skills taught.

Feedback From Participants to Trainers

Feedback is the breakfast of champions.

KEN BLANCHARD, *The One Minute Manager*

B ecoming an effective trainer is an ongoing lifetime quest. Every training session is an opportunity to learn and become skilled at developing people.

- The most effective way for trainers to improve is to get feedback from participants. This can be done:
  ✓ Informally. Circulating with participants at breaks can be useful, particularly if the trainer probes participants as to how enjoyable, useful, and applicable the materials and process have been thus far.
  ✓ By responding to people during the class. As a matter of courtesy, people may not reveal their frustrations to the trainer, but they will probably show them through their body language—for example:
    —Failure to get eye contact might indicate annoyance.
    —Crossed arms and legs coupled with a frown might indicate disagreement.
    —Rolling of eyes might indicate disbelief.
    —Sitting back in the chair with hands behind one's head could indicate skepticism.
    —Constant yawning could indicate boredom (or a lack of oxygen).
- Failure to respond to nonverbal feedback can be fatal. You should:
  ✓ Ask the group if there is a problem.

✓ Share your observations of what is happening, and ask for confirmation.

✓ Ask the group for guidance as to what you can do to address the problem.

✓ Suggest that the module will be completed quickly and you will move on to something of greater interest.

✓ At the end of each training day, review the group's general satisfaction by getting people to complete a scorecard (see Exhibit 4). This information should be collated and summarized for the group before beginning on the next day. Proposed changes should be discussed and agreed to. This will demonstrate a customer focus and give people a sense of control over the process and content.

- At the end of the session, ask the group to complete a more extensive survey, which will address all aspects of the training: the trainer's effectiveness, the materials, venue, and precourse registration. It should include sections for people to explain why they rated the workshop as they did. This anecdotal information is a very useful tool. (See Exhibit 5.).

- The information from surveys should be collated and summarized. Action plans should be developed to address key issues.

- Maintain a score for each workshop and chart the trend over time to see whether your effectiveness is improving.

  ✓ Learning from participants will take place if you are open to feedback. If you become defensive or even arrogant, you will experience no improvement, and you will face ongoing difficulties in the classroom.

  ✓ Meet the manager or managers of the participants after a course (say, one month later) to discuss participants' informal observations and recommendations about the course.

Exhibit 4. Daily program or course evaluation.

Name: _____ Seminar: _____

Seminar Leader: _____ Today's Date: _____

A. *Method of Instruction*
    Circle one of the following: day 1, day 2 of the seminar
    How would you rate the presentation methods (where applicable)

	Very Effective	Quite Effective	Needs Improvement	Not Effective
Delivery techniques	____	____	____	____
Material	____	____	____	____
Attendees' participation	____	____	____	____
Use of teaching aids	____	____	____	____
Leader's content/ input	____	____	____	____
Workbook/reference material	____	____	____	____

B. *Presentation*
    In your opinion the presentation was:
    1. __ Elementary   __ Varied   __ Advanced   __ Just right
    2. __ Fast   __ Slow   __ Suitably paced __ Erratic
    3. __ Too detailed __ Too general __ Too theoretical __ Correct

C. *Reaction to Session as a Whole*
    Did the content of this session meet your expectations? If
    not, please explain.
    Very much so __   To a great extent __   To some extent __   Not at all __

    _____

    _____

D. *Please indicate why you feel some parts were less effective,
    and explain below. You may check more than one box.*
    __ Read material __ Inadequately prepared __ Boring __ Too formal
    __ Repetitious   __ Strayed from subject   __ No objectives stated
    EXPLANATION:

    _____

    _____

Source: Reprinted with permission of Waterloo Management Education Centre, Waterloo, Ontario.

Exhibit 5. Evaluation after the session.

You are my client, and I value your feedback. Please respond candidly to the following questions:

Please rate the workshop on each criterion listed below:

	Exceeded Expectations	Met Expectations	Needs Improvement	Not Applicable
A. Seminar Content				
Material organization	___	___	___	___
Presentation level	___	___	___	___
Practicality of material to my job	___	___	___	___
Quality of written materials	___	___	___	___
Small group activities	___	___	___	___
Visual aids	___	___	___	___
Presentation				
Presentation style	___	___	___	___
Speaker's knowledge of subject	___	___	___	___
Coverage of material clear	___	___	___	___
Response to questions	___	___	___	___

B. Suggestions for Improvement

_____

_____

_____

C. Other Comments

_____

_____

_____

D. Please indicate the rating that best reflects your overall evaluation of this session.

Excellent	Good	Fair	Poor
___	___	___	___

Feedback From the Trainer to Participants

People learn a lot by getting feedback when they've made progress, as well as when they haven't.

Negative Feedback

- Giving negative feedback can be destructive or constructive depending on how it's done. Here's how to do it professionally:
  - ✓ Do it soon. Waiting too long might cause the person some problem in remembering what happened.
  - ✓ Ask for an invitation. Rather than give unsolicited feedback, ask, "Would you be interested in my observations?" or "Could I give you some feedback?"
  - ✓ Provide the feedback in private if it could cause embarrassment.
  - ✓ If you have created a relaxed environment and people have asked for feedback, provide your comments with the class all present.
  - ✓ Focus on the problem, not the person. This is best done beginning with "I" rather than "you." For example, say, "I was upset when I noticed the attack on Jack," or "I don't think that Mary is being listened to."
  - ✓ Be specific. Give examples. Tell how many times you ob-

served the problem. Generalizing and talking in general terms with comments such as, "There was a lot of confusion," is less helpful than saying, "I didn't understand the point you were making."
- ✓ Get the trainee to confirm agreement to the problem. In this way, you will get a commitment to find a solution.
- ✓ Involve the person. Create a dialogue to show your interest in the person and your respect for his or her opinions.
- Ask the trainee for solutions, and listen closely. Only if you feel the person is way off base should you suggest alternatives. Try saying, "That sounds fine. Would you be interested in another approach?"
- Confirm your understanding by summarizing the discussion, preferably with a clear action plan describing how things will be done differently next time.

Positive Feedback

- Giving positive feedback is not as easy as it sounds. Here are the key principles:
  - ✓ Do it soon after you notice the improvement.
  - ✓ Do it only for an improvement, not for repeated satisfactory performance.
  - ✓ Tell the person or group specifically what you like.
  - ✓ Give the person or group encouragement to continue to improve.
- Although most positive feedback is verbal, it can be useful to provide recognition in other ways too:
  - ✓ A pat on the back
  - ✓ Thumbs up
  - ✓ Showing the "OK" sign.
  - ✓ Nodding and making eye contact

Flip Chart Do's and Don'ts

The correct use of your equipment will enhance how your trainees perceive you and the effectiveness of your message.

- Here's how to make the best use of a flip chart:
  ✓ Write in bold, capital letters.
  ✓ Use dark colors for words—black or dark blue is best—and alternate the colors for each point when doing a long list.
  ✓ Number each point for easy reference.
  ✓ Use colors for highlighting, underlining, and bullets.
  ✓ Emphasize headings by writing them larger, using a different color, or underlining.
  ✓ Keep one idea per page.
  ✓ Post key ideas on the walls for easy reference.
  ✓ Precut masking tape, and stick the pieces on the legs of the flip chart stand. Use them to post pages on the walls. Put the tape on the side of the pages, not the top, so all you have to do is tear and post.
  ✓ Use diagrams and flowcharts to increase understanding.
  ✓ Add pictures where possible. Remember that a picture says a thousand words!
  ✓ Add reminders of the points you want to make by writing them in pencil on the appropriate flip chart page. You will be able to see the information, but your audience won't. They will be astonished at your familiarity with so many facts and figures.
  ✓ If you want to refer back to a particular page without thumbing through all the pages, consider attaching a label to key pages. You can (1) put a masking tape tab with details written on it or (2) color-code certain topics so that related subjects have a single color.
  ✓ If you're going to draw a model or diagram, predraw it in light pencil (so only you can see it).
  ✓ Always print clearly.

- Here are some don'ts:
  - ✓ Don't block the flip chart when you are writing on it. Stand to the side.
  - ✓ Don't talk at the flip chart as you are writing on it.
  - ✓ Avoid using markers made from strong chemicals. The writing may bleed through the flip chart paper.
  - ✓ Beware of using red or green; 7 percent of the population is color-blind and have trouble distinguishing these colors.

Games in Training

Games are used often in training sessions to demonstrate specific teaching principles through highly participative and nonthreatening exercises. Games work best when they use tools and techniques that are not related to the participants' working environment.

- There are many games available, in packaged formats and in specialized training guides.
- In selecting or designing games, ensure that any game is consistent with adult learning principles.
- Games should encourage healthy and humorous competition, which should acknowledge winners but never denigrate losers.
- Target games to the maturity and comfort level of the participants (not everyone likes to be blindfolded).
- Games should be directly related to a specific teaching principle in the lesson plan rather than to generic principles or observations.
- Ensure that the game is reasonably unique or novel for the participants. Many people have already been through simulated survival exercises.
- The intended outcomes or conclusions should not be predictable or obvious from the outset (e.g., that ten hands works faster than two hands).
- If the group is being divided into teams, make sure that the teams are small enough so all members can participate.
- Instructions should be clearly stated or written. Constant requests for clarification detract from the energy of the learning opportunties.
- The learning observations should refer to the process as well as the outcome.
- Allow ample time for debriefing the learning outcomes.
- Ensure that the time alloted for the game is adequate; otherwise the learning will be compromised by clock watching.

Here are some suggestions for games that relate to some typical course objectives.

- Team work practices
  - ✓ Use puzzles or crosswords that are missing some important pieces or clues. This game encourages listening and questioning skills at the same time as it demonstrates the importance of collaboration.
  - ✓ Charge each group with the task of designing the "perfect" restaurant menu (or holiday resort). During the debriefing, have groups discuss how they arrived at consensus and handled differences.
- Time management techniques
  - ✓ As a variation on standard "in-basket" exercises, design a list of activities that describe preparations for a vacation or spring house cleaning, and ask participants to prioritize the list.
  - ✓ Hand out copies of the daily newspaper, and give each participant ten minutes to prepare a one-page summary of the news. The participants who prepared the most concise yet comprehensive summaries then describe their methods.
- Customer service
  - ✓ Have participants lunch at a local fast-food restaurant. Have each person report back on the most and least appealing features of the service they received. Compare and discuss preferences and differences.
  - ✓ Have three or four participants draw up a list of features for their perfect car. Divide the class into sales teams who interview each "buyer." Compare how long it takes each team to develop the buyer profiles.
- Brainstorming and creativity exercises
  - ✓ Give each team some modeling clay. Ask them to design a sculpture that represents a particular theme (e.g., freedom, love).
  - ✓ Cut out pictures of products from a magazine. Ask each team to design an advertising slogan for each product.

Humor

The appropriate use of humor in training will get people relaxed and add to their enjoyment of the process. Here are some guidelines for using humor.

- Do:
  - ✓ Use stories that are funny and that illustrate a teaching point you are covering.
  - ✓ Use self-deprecating humor.
- Don't:
  - ✓ Use humor at any person's or group's expense or that embarrasses the organization.
  - ✓ Use humor that can be construed as racist or sexist in any way. Even in an all-male group, referring to women in a sexist manner will demonstrate a lack of professionalism and undermine your credibility.
  - ✓ Tell jokes if you are not good at it. It will cause you embarrassment and increase tension.
- You need not rely solely on your own sense of humor or repertoire of jokes to establish a sense of ease or relaxation. Here are some ways to introduce some fun without performing:
  - ✓ Invite participants to start the session or a new module with their own best joke, and award a prize based on a group rating.
  - ✓ Establish an inventory of comic strips on overheads that can gently poke fun at certain common or organization occurrences.
  - ✓ Have participants talk about their worst customer service experience or "bad boss" stories if they relate to the lesson (rule out any experiences that refer to the current organization).
  - ✓ Have participants volunteer to describe their worst gaffe in trying to use a specific skill being taught. Give out a prize for the "best" gaffe.
  - ✓ Be on the lookout for quotes that point out certain absurdities about workplace behavior. Start a session or a module

with an overhead with the appropriate quote, or include it in the training materials.

✓ Use videos that have some sophisticated humor built into the teaching principles.

✓ Hand out articles that have some humorous observations about certain workplace practices (e.g., "What I Shouldn't Have Learned at My Corporate Retreat").

✓ Consider case studies or role plays that include certain behavior that participants can laugh at and identify with.

✓ Use games that are sufficiently complex or intriguing to encourage participants to experiment with several different solutions. This typically causes people to laugh at some of their misguided attempts.

Icebreakers

Icebreakers help people relax and become receptive to learning. Here are some ideas to do it right.

- Not all icebreakers work. Some might bomb and cast a shadow on the rest of your training day. To avoid an exercise that increases tension and apprehension, consider the following:
  - ✓ Don't do anything that would cause you discomfort or annoyance if *you* were a participant.
  - ✓ Adjust the length of the icebreaker to suit the length of the session. A more extensive icebreaker would work for a workshop that lasts two to five days, whereas a quick exercise (of two to five minutes) would be appropriate for a session of one day or less.
  - ✓ Know your audience. Not all adults are ready to do something a little silly early on in the workshop. Generally, the more senior that people are, the less they might want to do anything that puts them at risk of looking foolish.
  - ✓ People's dress might give you a clue as to how much participants will engage in risky activities early on in the session. The rule is to play it more conservatively with people in business suits, and expect people who are casually dressed to stretch.
  - ✓ People who know each other may find some exercises redundant. A mixed audience of people from different organizations would benefit more from getting to know more about each other.
  - ✓ In-house workshops require less risky icebreakers than those taking place at a resort.
- Learning that deals with "soft" subjects such as conflict and communications benefits more from an icebreaker than one that has a focus on learning computer software.
- Participants who work with people might enjoy a more unusual exercise than participants with limited personal contact in their jobs.

- Examples of some low-risk icebreakers include:
  - ✓ Having people introduce themselves
  - ✓ Creating two-person teams and asking the partners to introduce the other by name, job, learning objectives, and something unusual about the person
  - ✓ Having people describe their most unusual training experience
  - ✓ Adding up the total years of business experience of all the participants, a great way to point out the opportunity to learn from each other
- More adventurous and time-consuming icebreakers include:
  - ✓ A team simulation that shows the value of working together
  - ✓ A scavenger hunt in which people are given a list of unusual statements about people. They then need to approach most people in the room to match the statement (e.g., "Has seven kids and eight cats") with the person. To encourage mixing, a prize can be awarded to the first person to complete the exercise.

Impact in the Classroom

Training isn't theater, but adding a little drama can increase the audience's attention during a session and aid retention afterward. The following suggestions will add impact to sessions.

- Invite senior executives to drop by unannounced for informal question-and-answer sessions.
- Hand out personalized letters from the company president to all participants at the beginning of the session, outlining his or her expectations for the course and for active participation.
- Videotape a breakout session, and play it later in the course. Have participants comment on learning styles and teamwork after watching the tape.
- Have participants nominate "winners" at the end of sessions (e.g., best contributor, most helpful, best team player, best sense of humor). Give out business books or other prizes.
- During customer service courses, have participants prepare a report card about the quality of service received during meals throughout the course. Use specific observations to emphasize key teaching lessons.
- Invite previous participants to the classroom to discuss how they applied specific principles they learned from the course.
- During lengthy courses, let participants spend an afternoon in a local library to compile a bibliography of books related to the course content.
- At the end of a course, have participants develop a learning contract with a buddy for follow-up after the course.
- At the end of the course, have one group develop a true-or-false quiz about the teaching principles for the rest of the group to answer.
- At the end of the course, do a composite portrait of all the best attitudes and actions of participants that contributed to the

success of the course. Send the summary out to everyone afterward.

- Involve the group in competitive intelligence exercises. Have group members interview family and friends to understand how other companies cope with issues that are highlighted during training.
- Do some open-book exercises. Have business articles and contemporary management books on hand so that participants can do some hands-on research about business issues and practices.
- Using games such as Scrabble or Pictionary, let participants compete as teams to demonstrate and reinforce the dynamics of group decision making.
- Use self-assessment exercises as often as possible. Few people can resist the impulse to discover more about themselves.
- Use current recruitment ads to demonstrate the kinds of characteristics and qualifications that management and leadership positions require. Relate this information to your own organization.
- Use someone from your organization's advertising department to lead the group in a brainstorming session and to talk about creative brainstorming techniques.
- To focus a discussion, use examples of obvious bloopers that other companies have made. Let participants contribute examples from their own experiences.
- Invite selected customers to talk about their expectations for the organization.
- Invite an industry expert to discuss contemporary issues over lunch.

Internet and Intranet

The Internet is a vast computer system that links computers worldwide. An intranet is a system that links all the computers within a given organization, sometimes including partners, such as suppliers.

Trainers should use every method available to them to communicate with clients. The Internet and intranets, increasingly popular forms of sharing information, can provide astonishing new opportunities to trainers to do more with less, providing flexibility and accessibility to learners.

- Trainers can set up home pages with course outlines and background materials for each program on the Internet and on an intranet. The following benefits accrue to the trainees:
  - ✓ They will be able to review background material at a time and place convenient to them.
  - ✓ They can get information without waiting.
  - ✓ The cost of transmission for those already using the technology is low.
  - ✓ Information will be current, as updating can be done easily and cheaply.
  - ✓ There will be less time spent in the classroom, as some information will already be known.
  - ✓ They have ability to review information efficiently.
  - ✓ They can share information and ideas, and answer questions easily.
  - ✓ There is easy access and support for people who are located far from the main training centers.
  - ✓ There will be an increased confidence booster for trainees as a consequence of having time to prepare for workshops by accessing information ahead of time.
- A training department using the Internet or intranet can:
  - ✓ Conduct a needs analysis.
  - ✓ Establish a Web page to advertise courses with details about the program objectives, course outline, location, and facilitator's credentials.

✓ Register people electronically.

✓ Enable participants to access materials instantly (particularly useful to those in remote locations).

✓ Review materials in advance and arrive at sessions better prepared.

✓ Reduce classroom time because people are better prepared, thereby using resources more effectively.

✓ Improve training effectiveness by enabling people to be more focused.

✓ Survey people about their subject matter knowledge before the start of the class, to allow for increased tailoring.

✓ Survey people after the class as to whether they have put the skills into practice.

✓ Set up conferencing dialogue to conduct postprogram dialogues on the use and application of course concepts. People can also mentor one another.

Keeping Trainees in the Classroom

Whether a course is held as a public forum or at an employee's worksite, all facilitators acknowledge that keeping trainees inside the training room is a chronic challenge. Today's technology—cellular phones, pagers, beepers—exacerbates the challenge by increasing the likelihood of distractions.

There are three reasons that trainees excuse themselves from training:

1. Business emergencies (clients, bosses, or colleagues contact them)
2. Personal emergencies (family illness, midday appointments)
3. Boredom (trainees may plead business or personal emergencies)

Here are some techniques for minimizing trainee exodus and time lost to catch-up training:

Prior to the Workshop

- Speak to participants before the class, particularly if it is being done on-site, to discuss the importance of staying in the class throughout the course. Stress:
  - ✓ The problem of gaps in their learning if they leave.
  - ✓ The possibility of letting their teammates down in group activities.
  - ✓ The creation of a precedent for others who might feel tempted to leave at will.
  - ✓ The importance of demonstrating commitment to the program.
  - ✓ How people might question their organization skills and ability to delegate.

- Speak to the participants' managers. Seek their support to:
  - ✓ Cover for the trainee.
  - ✓ Not bother the trainee about minor issues.
  - ✓ Stress the importance of the program to the trainee.

At the Workshop

- *Always* start the course on time. This is a clear message that tardiness after breaks and lunch will not be rewarded by late starts.
- Start the course by discussing a code of conduct for interruptions. Involve trainees in identifying what are legitimate excuses.
- Recruit a senior manager to kick off the course to emphasize the importance of professional behavior.
- Secure group consensus about the use of cellular phones and pagers.
- Identify exactly when breaks will occur, and stick to those times.
- Set up a message board outside the classroom.
- If interruptions are likely (for genuine business contingencies), set rules for participants' reentry to the classroom.
- Make yourself available at lunch breaks for catch-up exercises for those who had to leave briefly.
- Designate learning buddies who are accountable for catch-up information if their buddies must come and go.
- Monitor group energy and interest; take five-minute time-outs if interest is waning.
- Set an incentive for no interruptions (e.g., finishing a half-hour earlier than scheduled).
- Change the composition of breakout teams regularly during the day. New teammates can be energizing.
- Ensure that there is frequent group participation; one-way discussions can be boring.
- Use videos (one for each half-day session) to generate renewed interest and discussion.
- Invite executives to drop in during the day, and let trainees know they're coming. Most trainees like their supervisors to see them actively involved in learning.

- Stick to the agenda to reinforce a sense of professionalism in the classroom.
- Consider creative venues for breakout exercises (e.g., out of doors, hotel restaurants, company stock rooms). A change of scene can counter boredom.
- Close the session with a special guest or corporate executive.
- Suggest that trainees ask for the group's permission to leave the room for things other than rest room breaks. (This may not work in all cases; some people might find this approach childish.)
- Trainees are more inclined to be timely when they feel that they are learning. A trainer can show their interest in the amount of learning taking place. Here's one way to do it:
  - ✓ Put a piggy bank in front of each person or one at each table.
  - ✓ Give each person twenty pennies.
  - ✓ Ask people to put a penny in the piggy bank each time they learn something new or interesting.
- Giving people the assurance that their needs will be met is an added inducement to stay. You can do this by:
  - ✓ Leaving a blank page on the wall, called *Parking Lot*, in which issues unrelated to your topic are listed for discussion at a specified time
  - ✓ Giving each person sticky notes to write questions on. These can be put on a flip chart page, prominently displayed

Learning Contracts

A learning contract is an understanding, either written or verbal, that binds the learner to the accomplishment of specific learning goals.

- A comprehensive learning contract should state:
  - ✓ Key learning objectives.
  - ✓ Dates when subcomponents will be completed.
  - ✓ The resources to use.
  - ✓ Times when the training will take place.
  - ✓ The pace at which the training will be conducted.
  - ✓ The process to be used.
- Key benefits of a contract are that it will:
  - ✓ Induce learners to think through what they will learn.
  - ✓ Force trainees to identify how they will measure the outcome.
  - ✓ Produce written evidence of the trainees' commitment, for later evaluation and feedback.
  - ✓ Require learners to take a more active role to secure appropriate outcomes.
  - ✓ Enable the trainer to act in a facilitative rather that a transmitter role.
  - ✓ Give learners additional input into the content, process, time, and place, promoting additional commitment.
  - ✓ Make learners more self-directed, which could have other benefits for other projects that they may undertake with a greater sense of ownership.
- At the beginning of each workshop, ask learners to:
  - ✓ Take responsibility for what they learn.
  - ✓ Get involved and volunteer whenever possible. The more they practice the skills, the greater their ability will be to use them later.
  - ✓ Keep the trainer in touch with their needs. If their needs change, they should let the trainer know.
  - ✓ Support their ideas. They may not always agree with the

trainer, but differences of opinion will make the workshop more challenging and lively.

✓ Take care of their physical needs when they occur. (Of course, time will be set aside for refreshments, smoking, and rest room needs.)

✓ Keep the sessions on time. This is an important discipline in all good meetings and workshops. Once all have agreed on times, stick to them.

✓ Give everyone their full attention, and try not to call the office. Chances are that if they do, some issue there will break their attention. The body will still be here, but the mind will be back in the office.

✓ Enjoy themselves. Learning is most effective if they relax and have fun. This does not mean that they need not be serious about the subject matter.

Learning Organizations

The ability to learn faster than your competitors may be the only sustainable competitive advantage.

ARIE DE GEUS

A learning organization is one that recognizes the desire of people to learn and grow and provides them with that opportunity in order to enhance the future of the organization.

- In his groundbreaking book, *The Fifth Discipline*, Peter Senge identifies five principles that characterize a learning organization:
  - ✓ Systems thinking
  - ✓ Personal mastery
  - ✓ Mental models
  - ✓ Shared vision
  - ✓ Team learning
- These principles translate into three key practices that enable an organization to promote and support continuous learning:
  - ✓ The ability to learn from each other
  - ✓ The ability to learn from personal experience
  - ✓ The ability to learn from the system (i.e., organization successes and failures)
- There are three sets of variables that promote or reduce the learning experience:
  - ✓ Conditions
  - ✓ Activities
  - ✓ Results

Conditions

- A learning organization is not created overnight after a sudden shift in management philosophy. It evolves out of a systematic effort to develop a broad range of human resourcing practices.

- Hiring practices must test for demonstrated learning aptitude in the past and enthusiasm about continuous learning.
- Promotion decisions must acknowledge a candidate's contribution to personal and team learning.
- Compensation strategies must reward new skill acquisition with incentives that are directly tied to learning practices and results.
- The profile of managers includes and stresses coaching and mentoring responsibilities.
- Job design and organization divisions must be reviewed regularly to ensure that staff understand their role in contributing to the organization's success.
- Performance measurement systems must identify learning opportunities, as well as intended results.
- Business plans and organization goals must include the principle of continuous learning as a competitive lever.
- Training tools and courses should include opportunities for informal and self-directed learning.

Activities

- There are many informal activities that create a learning organization—for example:
  - ✓ Continuous feedback: team members to each other, managers to employees, and employees to managers.
  - ✓ Open communications practices that encourage suggestions
  - ✓ Opportunities to celebrate successes
  - ✓ Opportunities to share results within and among groups
  - ✓ Regular postmortems about what was done well, what went wrong, and what can be done better
  - ✓ The use of experiments as a tool for learning
  - ✓ Establishing and refining benchmarks for all important organization processes
  - ✓ Setting goals for teams, as well as individuals
  - ✓ Ensuring that employees have both the information and the tools to maximize their productivity

✓ Involving employees in setting measurements and evaluating results

Results

- Measuring and reporting results is itself a fundamental learning opportunity. To maximize this opportunity, consider the following:
  ✓ Report important results weekly; use e-mail and voice-mail systems for immediacy.
  ✓ Hold senior management forums regularly to analyze results; encourage open Q&A with employees.
  ✓ Communicate results in the context of changing internal, external, and global conditions.
  ✓ Use charts and diagrams in reporting results.
  ✓ Recognize successful coaches and mentors in public.
  ✓ Design learning graphs for key success indicators, and measure progress regularly.
  ✓ Summarize informal and anecdotal feedback about learning outcomes to be included with formal results.

Lesson Plan Development

A course without a lesson plan is like a map without a scale. Trainers who follow a clear lesson plan can develop course content that has a specific relationship to the organization's requirements, meets specific skill gaps, and relates teaching principles to the content of the learning experience.

- Both seasoned trainers and line managers are often required to create a lesson plan as a first step in designing a training session, either from scratch or by refining existing training materials.
- A lesson plan is *not:*
  - ✓ A course description for a training catalog.
  - ✓ An advertising circular.
  - ✓ A facilitator's guide.
- A lesson plan is a summary of course outcomes, teaching principles, and methods that links a training lesson to business planning.
- A lesson plan includes the following components:
  - ✓ Learning objectives
  - ✓ Target audience
  - ✓ Course prerequisites
  - ✓ Key teaching principles
  - ✓ Teaching methodology
  - ✓ Delivery time lines
  - ✓ Materials

Learning Objectives

- Learning objectives should be expressed as outcomes for the participants and should use action verbs (e.g., "At the end of this session, participants will be able to . . .").
- Most courses should have three or four specific outcomes. A

single outcome is typically too general to be useful in planning specific training.

- Examples of learning outcomes for a course are:
  - ✓ To recognize selling opportunities.
  - ✓ To clarify customer needs.
  - ✓ To cut meeting times by 50 percent.

Target Audience

- Most courses address specific skill gaps.
- Participants should be identified in terms of a specific level of competence required for certain operating principles or practices (e.g., "First-line managers who must carry out performance evaluations consistent with established standards").

Course Prerequisites

- Many courses build on other teaching lessons in related or preparatory courses (e.g., "The feedback principles will build on lessons in the coaching modules"). Previous courses or experience levels should be identified clearly.

Key Teaching Principles

- Teaching principles are the building blocks to stated course outcomes (e.g., "The use of open questions as an aid to probing customer concerns").
- Teaching principles identify the context for using the newly acquired skills.

Teaching Methodology

- There are many ways to demonstrate key teaching principles. Examples of teaching methodologies are:
  - ✓ Group exercises.
  - ✓ Brainstorming exercises.

✓ Team activities.
✓ Role plays.
✓ Case studies.
✓ Simulations.

Delivery Time Lines

- Time lines are the allocated time needed to teach the specific principles.
- Time lines are typically organized into modules of related points (e.g., Feedback Principles, 2 hours; Introduction to Coaching, 2 hours; Conducting a Performance Interview, 4 hours).

Materials

- Materials include:
    ✓ Participant guides or workbooks.
    ✓ Trainer reference materials.
    ✓ Videos.
    ✓ Overheads.

Linking Training to Business Needs

There is only one measure of training's effectiveness: Did an important change occur that is directly related to an organization's ability to meet its business goals?

- To evaluate training, one can differentiate between programs that teach *skills* and those that convey *information*. Group sessions that deliver information (such as policy changes, statistical information, or organization priorities) are not training sessions; they are communication forums.
- Business-based training links a change in skill level to business objectives. Training outcomes must demonstrate a direct relationship to indicators of performance:
  - ✓ Quality
  - ✓ Timeliness
  - ✓ Cost-effectiveness
  - ✓ Satisfaction
- Training outcomes can be divided into two types of change:
  - ✓ New business challenges
  - ✓ An opportunity to correct business inefficiencies
- Examples of new business challenges include opportunities to:
  - ✓ Penetrate new markets.
  - ✓ Lower production costs.
  - ✓ Increase the speed of service.
- Examples of opportunities to correct business inefficiencies include:
  - ✓ A large number of customer complaints.
  - ✓ Unusually high staff turnover caused by poor management practices.
  - ✓ Repairs resulting from equipment failure.
- Standard courses, such as leadership training and time management, may be about either opportunity or corrections. For example:

- ✓ Leadership training that is intended to increase staff productivity is an *opportunity*. Leadership training that is held as a result of specific employee complaints is a *correction*.
- ✓ Time management training that upgrades current skills is an *opportunity*. Time management training that is in response to deviations from set standards is a *correction*.
- There are four principles to identify the relationship of training to a business's need:
  - ✓ *Understanding the business plan*. The business plan refers to organization or department goals that will be either strengthened or compromised by the training.
  - ✓ *Determining who the client is*. The client is the manager who "owns" the business plan and is accountable for its successful implementation.
  - ✓ *Qualifying and quantifying the change required*. The change required is determined by assessing the competence of the trainees and comparing it with the desired performance.
  - ✓ *Assessing the likelihood that changes related to training can be implemented*. The likelihood is related to specific conditions and factors that will affect the trainees' opportunity to use the new skills.
- A training plan that overlooks any of the four elements cannot demonstrate business-based results, no matter how effective the material or the presentation.
- Business-based training must be prioritized in order to maximize its impact on organization goals.
- Three elements of setting priorities for training are:
  - ✓ Size of skill gap. The size of the skill gap can be evaluated by determining how much change is needed to meet operational standards.
  - ✓ Urgency to close a skill gap. Urgency refers to the deadline for making changes to operating standards through a training initiative.
  - ✓ Impact of closing a skill gap. Impact refers to the dollars and time saved or the increased effectiveness that the training initiative can generate.
- When you must make important decisions about what training initiatives should take precedence in your organization, fill out the chart in Exhibit 6 as accurately as you can to aid you in understanding what your training priorities are.

Exhibit 6 will help identify the situations that have the greatest potential to effect significant change. Training 100 people for a low-urgency gap may have significantly less impact than training 10 people who can implement significant change quickly.

Exhibit 6. Priority analysis grid.

Skill Gap	High	Medium	Low
Size			
Urgency			
Impact			

Measuring Training Results

Training needs and benefits are often described in anecdotal terms, but training dollars need to be justified like any other expenditures.

- Measuring training results is a process that describes:
  - ✓ The current competence level.
  - ✓ The required competence level.
  - ✓ Time frame for results.
  - ✓ Costs of results.
- Examples of current competency levels that are measurable are:
  - ✓ Documented error rates.
  - ✓ Time required to complete specific tasks.
  - ✓ Complaints from customers about delays or personal service attitudes.
  - ✓ Complaints from staff about supervisory practices.
  - ✓ Equipment malfunctions related to inexperience.
  - ✓ Noncompliance or infractions of government policies.
- Determining competence is not easy. These indicators can help managers to quantify competence levels:
  - ✓ Amount of time supervisors invest in coaching and monitoring employees
  - ✓ Employee motivation and interest in assuming new tasks
  - ✓ The number of outcomes generated by teams
  - ✓ Productivity figures that have changed significantly compared to results in previous years
  - ✓ Competitors' productivity figures
  - ✓ External benchmarks for similar processes
  - ✓ Employee attitude surveys and training needs analyses
  - ✓ Observations and recommendations recorded in performance appraisals
  - ✓ Opportunities to practice new skills
- Competence is difficult to quantify for wide-scale training ini-

tiatives that focus on promoting large-scale change, such as organizationwide reengineering or the creation of a vision and mission. For these cases, identify one or two key outcomes that can be used as a reference for determining current competence levels.

Required Competence Levels

- The required level of competence will be expressed in the same quantifiable measurements as current competence levels.
- In order to establish realistic expectations, consider:
  - ✓ Business plan requirements. Are certain standards expected in order to meet the needs of customers?
  - ✓ The degree of expertise an employee should demonstrate with little supervision.
  - ✓ Internal and external customer expectations.
  - ✓ The opportunity employees have to practice new skills or techniques.
  - ✓ Incentives for employees to practice new skills or techniques.
  - ✓ Potential barriers to effective performance of new skills, such as unclear operating procedures or poor equipment.

The Time Frame for Achieving Results

- Training results are not instantaneous. As a general rule of thumb, the greater the long-term impact of the training results, the longer the time frame for measuring results.
- Here are some guidelines for setting meaningful time frames for measuring results:
  - ✓ Regular reports that describe production and error rates
  - ✓ Operational requirements that specify important improvement deadlines
  - ✓ The period of time in which previous training resulted in meaningful improvements
  - ✓ Other conditions (tools, coaching, opportunity) that will have an impact on the use of new skills

✓ The length of time participants have been in their current position

Costs for Achieving Meaningful Results

- The cost of the results of training over a period of time has multiple components—among them:
  ✓ The costs of facilitation.
  ✓ Course design costs.
  ✓ Facilities costs.
  ✓ Materials costs (workbooks, videos, training aids).
  ✓ Travel and accommodations costs for facilitators or trainees, or both.
  ✓ Time off the job for trainees (lost production time or missed opportunities).
  ✓ Dedicated equipment for practice or experimentation.
- The total cost of a training initiative should be assessed against the expected quantifiable results in order to derive a cost-benefit statement. If the costs exceed the expected benefits, determine which costs can be reduced.
- When assessing training results, consider also the hidden costs that contribute to results:
  ✓ Supervisory time in helping staff implement new skills
  ✓ Reassignment of newly trained employees to positions that do not require the use of recently learned skills
  ✓ The introduction of new equipment or processes that makes new skills obsolete

Mentoring

There is always room at the top.

DANIEL WEBSTER

Mentoring programs are an ideal way for organizations to encourage individuals to take responsibility for their long-term development. At the same time, mentors can increase their coaching, feedback, and leadership skills. The organization will gain all around.

Here are suggestions and guidelines suggested by organizations that have implemented successful mentor programs.

- Set budget guidelines for the program since there will be costs for orientation sessions, self-assessment guides, and program publicity.
- Remember to estimate the hidden costs of a program (e.g., time off the job, travel costs).
- Determine who can participate in the program as mentors and mentees.
- Decide whether the relationships will be one on one or involve more than one mentee per mentor.
- Consider how the matching will be done after doing research on some successful mentor programs.
- Set time limits for evaluating results. Research suggests that one year is the optimum time frame for evaluating results.
- Mentors should be at least two levels higher than a mentee so mentees have the advantage of senior perspective.
- Develop a workbook or seminar that allows mentees to do comprehensive self-assessment about goals, as well as their individual strengths and weaknesses.
- Create formal contracts between mentors and mentees that include time commitments.

- Determine appropriate recognition and incentives for mentors (e.g., Mentor of the Year award).
- Provide forums for mentors to meet with each other for sharing suggestions and successes. Do the same for mentees.
- Be sure to publicize successes and outcomes to keep the momentum strong.
- Ideal mentees are people who:
  - ✓ Establish a small number of long-term goals that are specific, measurable, achievable, realistic, and time based.
  - ✓ Set some key steps that will need to be taken to achieve long-term goals and dates by when they will be complete.
  - ✓ Make a public commitment to their goals, so that others can monitor and encourage the mentee.
  - ✓ Spend a few minutes each day visualizing the attainment of goals.
  - ✓ Find one thing that they can learn from someone they work with.
  - ✓ Do one thing each day that will take them closer to their goal.
  - ✓ Set goals that are important to themselves, as much as they may please others.
  - ✓ Treat failure as an opportunity to learn.
  - ✓ Keep track of the most important lessons learned so that they can be referred to in order to reinforce continuous learning.
  - ✓ Learn to listen to and accept negative feedback as an opportunity to learn.
  - ✓ Keep their goals in front of them constantly (e.g., posted on a mirror at home or in a desk drawer).
  - ✓ Approach each day with a sense of discovery.
  - ✓ Take more risks.
  - ✓ Keep a list of things that it would be good to learn within five, ten and twenty years
- Mentors can contribute to the development process in many different ways, including:
  - ✓ Allowing the mentee to observe senior management meetings.
  - ✓ Taking the mentee to professional networking meetings.
  - ✓ Reviewing the mentee's resumé for critical comment.
  - ✓ Passing on topical articles and books for comment.

- ✓ Discussing the impact of their own role models and mentors.
- ✓ Passing on invitations to professional development events such as breakfast meetings and product launches.
- Mentoring meetings are most successful when they follow a set format:
  - ✓ Updates on action items
  - ✓ Debriefing on problematic assignments since the last meeting
  - ✓ Feedback by the mentor on his or her observations of the mentee in action
  - ✓ Suggestion for development initiatives, including reading and industry events
  - ✓ Opportunity for the mentee to share success stories
  - ✓ Mutual "homework" assignments that cover both research and action items
- Regular meetings between mentor and mentee will be productive if:
  - ✓ There is a focus on one area of development.
  - ✓ The meeting ends with "homework" assignments.
  - ✓ Both sides practice careful listening.
  - ✓ Time restrictions are honored.
- Exhibit 7 is a survey that can be used to measure the success of individual mentor-mentee relationships specifically and the program in general.

Exhibit 7. Mentoring survey.

Instructions to the Mentee
Circle the one response that best describes your feelings about the mentoring process.

1 = strongly disagree; 2 = disagree; 3 = neither agree nor disagree; 4 = agree; 5 = strongly agree

	Strongly Disagree				*Strongly Agree*

Advocate

• The mentor represents my interests at the senior level.	1	2	3	4	5
• The mentor assists in getting me assignments that give me exposure at a senior level.	1	2	3	4	5

Coach

• The mentor helps me to set challenging goals.	1	2	3	4	5
• The mentor gives me appropriate feedback in relation to my goals.	1	2	3	4	5

Role Model

• The mentor demonstrates the behavior he or she expects of me.	1	2	3	4	5

Communications

• The mentor listens to me and respects my ideas.	1	2	3	4	5
• The mentor sets aside sufficient uninterrupted time to deal with my issues.	1	2	3	4	5
• The mentor shows sincere interest in my development	1	2	3	4	5

Exhibit 7. Continued.

Training

- The mentor provides me with
  useful ideas for my training and
  development.   1 2 3 4 5

Problem Solving

- The mentor encourages me to
  solve my own problems.   1 2 3 4 5
- The mentor makes suggestions
  only after I have tried to solve
  problems for myself.   1 2 3 4 5

Professional Development

- The mentor helps find
  professional organizations and
  contacts for me   1 2 3 4 5
- The mentor helps to link me with
  other mentees who can benefit
  from one another's experience
  and education   1 2 3 4 5

Methodology: Choosing the Right One

I t is possible to train people in all sorts of ways.

- Training can be grouped into two broad categories: self-directed or facilitated. Each has a variety of methods of presenting materials and ideas.
- Self-directed learning gives people the opportunity to take control of their own training. They decide what to learn, how to learn it, when to do it, and where.
- Self-directed learning can be done by:
  ✓ Individual research in books, magazines, and on the Internet.
  ✓ Self-paced manuals, tapes, and videos.
  ✓ Self-paced computer-based training, accessing information from floppy disks, CD-ROM, the Internet, or the organization's intranet.
- Courses that involve using and practicing techniques and processes (budgeting, equipment repair, project management) are better suited to self-directed training media, where the consistency of applying the learning is important.
- Trainer- or facilitator-directed learning gives participants limited control over the content and process of learning. This learning most often takes place in a classroom setting.
- Training courses that focus on learning and practicing skills that involve relationships with others (team, leadership, customer service) are better suited to facilitated learning. In these courses it is important to discuss reactions and previous experience as part of the learning process.
- Messages in facilitated learning are conducted in any one of the following methods:
  ✓ *Verbal.* This is probably the least effective way. Lecturing as

the sole medium of training leads to a retention of around 15 percent.

✓ *Visual.* People retain more when they see the message. An image is easier to recall than verbal messages. Visual images are conveyed through slides, overheads, and flip charts.

✓ *Video.* This method combines visual and verbal messages and is often an effective training tool, particularly if the message is short (under ten minutes) and demonstrations of what is right and wrong closely approximate the real world of the learner.

✓ *Role play.* This method requires the learner to practice a skill, such as conflict resolution or negotiating, after learning some theory. An observer monitors the role play and gives participants feedback on the extent to which they followed a model.

✓ *Simulation.* This is the creation of a situation closely akin to the real world, which enables people to be put into situations that produce behavior typically less than desirable. At the end of the exercise, the group debriefs and reviews the observations of participants, observers, and even video. The learning can be powerful. It can also be threatening and upsetting if feedback is not handled effectively.

✓ *Case study.* After learning points of theory, participants are given a case study to read and analzye. They can be given questions to answer, which will determine how effectively they applied the theory.

✓ *Group development.* This exercise is facilitated by an experienced person who enables the group to identify and deal with issues that are preventing them from performing at a high level.

• With the availability of multimedia tools and ever-increasing resource materials (books, videos), it is often advisable to conduct lengthy training sessions using a mix of tools as well as facilitated learning.

• Check with other organizations that may have tried certain training tools to get a realistic assessment of their effectiveness.

Minimizing Time off the Job

No matter how urgent the training, production and service requirements always seem more urgent. Here are some practices that can help you to reduce time in the classroom without jeopardizing training results.

- Consider holding classes between 10 A.M. and 3 P.M., rather than for a full day. By eliminating breaks and shortening a lunch hour, you can still complete the lesson plan and allow trainees to attend to urgent business.
- Use lunch hours for video presentations or executive visits during courses.
- Weekend seminars are becoming increasingly more popular. Include a group outing or banquet in the agenda to reduce the "pain" factor.
- Include real-life problems or policy planning exercises in the course material and case studies, so that the training produces bona-fide business outcomes.
- Team up with another company to share course costs, facilitators, and simulation equipment so that important courses can be held without depleting your employee ranks all at once.
- Share the time investment with employees for popular voluntary courses; hold the courses from 2 P.M. to 8 P.M.
- Develop a priority ranking for course content on evaluation forms. When time is tight, be prepared to drop the least useful modules.
- Reduce classroom time by developing comprehensive precourse materials and quizzes so that trainees can hit the ground running.
- Use take-home exercises during a course to shorten actual teaching time.
- Investigate training tools such as self-directed workbooks and computer-based training to replace generic skills training.

- Nominate subject matter experts to conduct informal "lunch-and-learn" sessions for short topics.
- Research the availability and quality of certain courses at community colleges or other postsecondary institutions, and encourage employee attendance through tuition reimbursement programs.
- Condense lengthy courses by identifying core topics, and use coaches or mentors to provide informal sessions for noncore topics.
- Use precourse testing to get a sense of the competence of the trainees. You may decide to shorten or delete certain topics as a result.
- Make sure that refresher training is just that; don't repeat an entire course if it isn't necessary.
- Be prepared to defer some training courses if too few people are available. Filling spaces with employees who may not need or use the training is a bad economic decision.

Needs Analysis

A training needs analysis will enable managers to anticipate and meet training needs in a timely and cost-effective manner. Here are some ideas to ensure that the process is effective and professional.

- A comprehensive training needs survey will contribute to the effectiveness of your training strategy by:
  - ✓ Setting training needs priorities.
  - ✓ Setting training budget guidelines.
  - ✓ Setting training delivery deadlines.
- To encourage participation in the survey and to solicit useful information, the survey document should be:
  - ✓ Anonymous and confidential.
  - ✓ Easy to read, with clear instructions and questions.
  - ✓ Relevant to the organization's unique operating challenges and conditions.

Here are some guidelines for designing a formal survey.

- Use multiple-choice and yes/no questions as often as possible to make it easier and quicker for employees to respond and to collate information.
- Ask very specific open questions—for example, about the person's most recent course, most useful course, and most urgent training need.
- Leave room for short comments after each major category of questions.
- Collect background information about employees, including:
  - ✓ Level of education.
  - ✓ Training history in previous organizations.
  - ✓ Length of service with the company.
  - ✓ Geographic location.
  - ✓ Major organization division.
  - ✓ Employee level within the organization (executive, manager, team member).

- Determine whether an employee is familiar with key training policies and practices, including:
  - ✓ Training catalogs and curriculum.
  - ✓ Training application forms and course registration procedures.
  - ✓ Educational assistance programs.
  - ✓ Performance appraisal system.
  - ✓ Training library or self-study facility.
- Use scales for describing a course's usefulness rather than narrative comments.
- Limit scales to 1–3, to elicit a specific opinion from survey participants.
- Differentiate between training needs for proficiency on the job and professional development needs for future positions.
- Solicit information about the need for both refresher and new courses.
- Do not repeat questions already addressed through post-course evaluations.
- Have participants identify specific barriers to training, as well as barriers to practicing skills gained through training.
- Use a 360° approach. What suggestions do participants have about their managers' and coworkers' training needs?
- Include questions about employees' interest in and availability for after-hours training.
- Do not assume that all employees are interested in promotion. Ask if, and when, an employee hopes to be promoted.
- Rate the effectiveness of other forms of training needs surveys (e.g., annual evaluations, managerial coaching, mentoring).
- Ask if employees are willing to contribute to or share the cost of certain kinds of training.
- Get information about ideal conditions for training delivery (e.g. on-site versus off-site, internal versus external facilitators).
- Limit the number of questions. Research demonstrates that the interest and energy level to provide accurate information decrease dramatically after twenty-five questions.
- You may interview a cross-section of managers, particularly the most influential. Ask them:
  - ✓ What are the key performance gaps?

✓ Which areas or levels of the organization should be focused
on?
- For ongoing training courses already identified, ask:
  ✓ Who needs the training?
  ✓ How many people need to be trained?
  ✓ What issues should the training resolve?
  ✓ When should the training be complete?
  ✓ How large is the budget?
- Once you have collected your information and formulated
  your plan, meet with key decision makers, and present your
  findings. Your report, oral or in writing, should cover:
  ✓ The problem.
  ✓ The cause.
  ✓ Recommended solution.
  ✓ Your action plan.
  ✓ The cost and benefit.
  ✓ Approvals required.

Needs Analysis: Using 360° Feedback

There are many ways to determine the key skills a person needs to improve. Few other methods are as good as the input from those with whom the individual interacts: their manager, peers, and direct reports. Here is a simple way to determine training needs.

- Create a list of skills that courses are aiming to improve.
- Develop a survey from the list. The survey could be done in one of two ways:
  - ✓ An *open-ended survey,* to allow people to provide a description of how much a particular employee needs to improve on the use of that skill(s) or is effective at using it
  - ✓ A *numerical ranking* using a scale of 1 to 10:

1	=	very poor
2.5	=	poor
5	=	average
7.5	=	competent
10	=	very competent

Some surveys use a five-point scale. This is less satisfactory when aggregating the scores of six to ten people who fill out the survey since one tends to lose the nuances that a larger score will highlight.

- Discuss or communicate the process to each trainee. Clarify important issues such as confidentiality—who sees the report.
- Give the survey to between six and ten people to complete for each potential trainee.
- Make sure that you get a good mix of people—manager, peers, and direct reports—so as not to bias your sample.
- Ensure that the survey is anonymous. Do not ask people to identify themselves by name on the survey.
- Aggregate the data so that all opinions are included.

- Meet with the potential trainee to discuss the report.
- Develop a plan that will address the trainee's key weaknesses.
- Involve the person's manager (if you are not that person) and mentor (if any) in the training plan. Ensure follow-up and appropriate recognition when trainees finish the program, and also down the road when they meet the goals set for the training.

Nervousness: Overcoming Butterflies

Some people are not comfortable talking in front of others, and many a speech has been destroyed by the resulting anxiety. Here are some techniques to help you reduce your butterflies. Remember: Everyone has some apprehensions before a speech. Some tension produces performance-enhancing adrenaline.

One Day Before Training

- Prepare, prepare, prepare. There are many things trainees will forgive; inadequate preparation is not one of them.
- Anticipate potential reactions or concerns and questions trainees will have.
- Learn as much as you can about the potential audience: their average skill level, demographics, and prior training experiences.
- Ask some of the trainees what will make the session successful from their point of view.
- Ask the client what he or she expects the training experience to achieve.
- Prepare index cards with key introductory information.

One Hour Before Training

- Check out the training room—its heating, seating, equipment, and lights.
- Test-drive the overhead projector, VCR, and any other equipment you will use.

- Walk around the room to get a sense of the trainees' perspective.
- Lay out your overheads in order, and line up marking pens and masking tape.
- Talk to everyone you run into, about anything. Don't make your introduction your first verbal foray of the day.
- Stop preparing. Last-minute reviews only heighten your sense of doom.
- Spend a few minutes alone before the presentation to collect your thoughts and focus your energy.
- Eliminate possible distractions on your person—for instance, bracelets that clang and loose change jiggling in your pocket.

Immediately Before the Session

- Shake hands with participants as they enter the room to reinforces the one-on-one relationship.
- Remind yourself that trainees are coming to learn, not to be impressed by your talent.
- Chat briefly with as many people as you can.
- Remind yourself that the group really does want you to succeed (have a little faith in human nature).
- Before you start, take a few deep breaths to regulate your breathing.

During the Introduction

- If you have a small audience, begin your presentation casually with a two-way discussion of something topical. This will reduce tension and allow you to ease into your speech.
- Be sincere. Don't overdo the enthusiasm, which can ring false.
- Make individual eye contact with as many people as possible at the start.
- Ignore advice that says you should always start with a joke. A flat joke is worse than a flat introduction. Do use humor if you feel comfortable doing so.
- Use cue cards instead of a written script. You will speak nor-

mally (with eye contact), and keep in touch with your audience.

- Be yourself. Emulating someone else will make you feel awkward, and the audience will react with skepticism.
- Maintain eye contact with a friendly face in the audience—someone who smiles or nods at you when you make a point. This positive feedback will increase your confidence and let you know how you are doing. Similarly, avoid eye contact with someone who is looking unhappy.
- Don't fiddle with a pointer, pen, change in your pocket, or anything else that may be handy. You will distract the audience.
- Visualize your audience in a nonthreatening way, such as sitting on a throne or with their underwear on! They will appear less threatening.
- Acknowledge that people come to training sessions with varying degrees of enthusiasm.
- If all else fails, acknowledge your nervousness briefly; point out that it is a mark of respect for your audience.
- Remember that it is mathematically impossible for one person to be smarter than the combined experience and resources of the group. You are there to leverage learning, not to outdo participants' skills and aptitudes.

On-the-Job Training

Training is a lot cheaper than ignorance. On-the-job training in technical, interpersonal, team, and business skills is a key component of any manager's duties. Here are some ideas to help.

- Determine what kind of training to give:
  - ✓ *Job rotation* will give associates a wider perspective and additional job skills.
  - ✓ *Cross-training* enables people to substitute for one another during temporary absences.
  - ✓ *Task forces* and other temporary problem-solving groups focus on customer service, process improvement, and product or service development.
  - ✓ *Delegation* of additional responsibilities enables people to learn more challenging tasks and increase their opportunities to demonstrate managerial talent.
- On-the-job training occurs in most workplaces, using the skills of experienced staff to transfer specific skills to a larger population.
- Informal on-the-job training is part of every manager's job. Including formal on-the-job training in a company's training plan has many advantages:
  - ✓ Formal recognition of the skills and talents of experienced staff.
  - ✓ Relating training to measurable, observable business outcomes.
  - ✓ The opportunity to practice new skills for sustained training results.
  - ✓ The use of equipment and other tools for hands-on learning.
  - ✓ The ability to measure trainees' progress and adjust the pace of instruction accordingly.
  - ✓ Flexibility in scheduling training to meet workplace demands.

✓ Lowered costs by conducting on-site training rather than using expensive training facilities.

✓ Feedback to managers about trainees' proficiency for follow-up coaching.

✓ The creation of a larger pool of trained employees as backups or successors for emergencies.

- Successful on-the-job training programs have these principles in common:

  ✓ Instructors are identified and trained in adult learning principles, facilitation techniques, and lesson plan creation.

  ✓ Learning objectives and expectations are clearly defined.

  ✓ Formal lesson plans are developed that include both theory and practice.

  ✓ Training materials are developed for trainees to use during and after the session.

  ✓ Time is set aside for the training.

  ✓ Trainees receive individual feedback about their progress.

  ✓ Evaluation forms are created for trainees to complete after the session.

  ✓ Formal train-the-trainer sessions are available.

- An effective training plan should include:

  ✓ Objectives for the session.

  ✓ A step-by-step outline of the learning lessons.

  ✓ Time allocation for both the overall session and each component.

  ✓ A list of resource materials, cross-referenced for each component.

  ✓ Identification of group and individual exercises.

- When you train people, walk the associate through four steps:

  ✓ Explain the task, why it needs to be done, and how it should be done.

  ✓ Demonstrate the task. If it is long and complex, break it down into bite sizes (modules) and sequences, doing one part at a time.

  ✓ Ask trainees to try the task while you observe them. Note things that they do well as well as mistakes.

  ✓ Give the trainees feedback. Praise any progress to increase their confidence. Be specific about what they did well.

- In the event that you notice a mistake, review your instructions through description and demonstration. Ask trainees to confirm their understanding of the task before trying it again.

- If you have demonstrated a task more than three times and the trainee has not yet learned it, consider breaking the task down even further. If this cannot be done or has already been done, it is likely that the trainee is not suited for the job.

- Establish the trainee's preferred method of learning: hearing, seeing, or doing. If it is difficult to decide the trainee's preferred method or you are training more than one person, use all three instruction methods.

- Here are the common mistakes made in the name of on-the-job training:

    ✓ *Setting impossible goals.* If you do this, the person will be focusing on failure rather than learning.

    ✓ *Focusing on punishment in the event of failure.* Failure can be an opportunity to learn. Don't develop a climate that will lead to paralysis.

    ✓ *Finding fault rather than success.* If you do this, you will create dishonesty because people will hide mistakes instead of dealing with them.

    ✓ *Hovering around while the trainee is practicing the skill.* Doing this indicates a lack of confidence in the trainee, which will become a self-fulfilling prophecy. The trainee will ask for help each time he or she encounters an obstacle instead of problem solving.

    ✓ *Overruling the trainee's decision.* Unless health and safety are compromised, think twice about countering an employee's decision. Let the person try an alternative approach. Maybe it will work better. If not, what the person could learn from failure could be worth the investment of extra time.

Orientation Programs

S tarting employees off on the right foot will help get them up to speed and contributing quickly. Here's how to do it successfully.

- Having hired the right person for the job, you can promote the new employee's successful adjustment into the organization by a thorough orientation.
- Your program design will be influenced by four factors:
  - ✓ *Budget*—how much money you have allocated to orientation
  - ✓ *Geography*—number of different geographic locations
  - ✓ *Volume*—number of new employees anticipated annually
  - ✓ *Feedback*—from employees who have attended previous orientation programs
- Here are some important do's for designing and conducting an orientation program:
  - ✓ Set standards for managers in orienting staff.
  - ✓ Make the program easy for all managers to deliver.
  - ✓ Stress the customers' perspective.
  - ✓ List and discuss your organization's main competitors.
  - ✓ Allow ample opportunities for new employees to ask questions.
  - ✓ Deliver at least some parts of the program on the first day a new employee joins the company.
  - ✓ Create information booklets or brochures with important information for reference during and after the session.
  - ✓ Consider the economics and usefulness of a new-employee info line.
- Here are some important don'ts to consider in designing and delivering an orientation program:
  - ✓ Don't set complicated follow-up schedules, they are difficult to maintain.
  - ✓ Don't create expensive corporate videos if company information is subject to change.

- ✓ Don't expect new employees to retain detailed information without printed reference material.
- ✓ Don't set unrealistic expectations and roles for your senior management team to deliver parts of the program if their schedules are subject to change.
- ✓ Don't delay the orientation program too long while waiting for a sizable group.
- Plan to ensure a successful integration of the new person:
  - ✓ Set up the new employee's workstation in advance.
  - ✓ Have someone greet the new employee on his or her arrival.
  - ✓ Post a notice on the bulletin board welcoming the employee and inviting others to do the same.
- Spend some time getting to know new associates. Learn about their work background, previous jobs, and likes and dislikes.
- Give the new associates information about the organization:
  - ✓ Company history
  - ✓ The marketplace for its products or services
  - ✓ Customer overview
  - ✓ Organization structure and key people
  - ✓ Company successes and challenges
  - ✓ Employee population
  - ✓ Standards of behavior
  - ✓ Performance standards, including hours of work
  - ✓ Documentation and information on salary and benefits
- Give new employees a tour of the facilities. Show them the key facilities, including the parking lot, rest rooms, the cafeteria, and emergency exits.
- Review the company's mission, values, and philosophy if these are available and documented. Discuss how the employees can contribute to the successful achievement of corporate goals.
- Show the new employees each department and how it relates to yours. Also show the major products and services. This information will give them the big picture so they can see how they fit.
- You can do some of the orientation yourself, but consider giving each new associate a partner from another work area. This has important benefits:
  - ✓ Suggests that departments work together

✓ Stresses teamwork
✓ Establishes contacts with people in other areas
✓ Improves communications between work areas
✓ Demonstrates your esteem for people outside your work area

- To facilitate new associates' integration into the social fabric of the company, provide a buddy who can act as a mentor when you are not available and be company during breaks.
- Do not prejudice new associates about other people or departments by running them down. Allow new employees to form their own opinions based on their experience.
- Establish an open-door policy so that associates have easy access to you when needed.
- Follow up regularly to see how new associates are doing. Praise their accomplishments to increase their confidence and sense of satisfaction at having joined the organization.
- Treat new associates as a resource. They will have a fresh perspective on ways of working. Be receptive to their ideas by showing your interest and, where possible, acting on their suggestions.
- Schedule a meeting about six weeks after the orientation to find out:
  ✓ How the person is doing.
  ✓ What more you can do to help.
  ✓ Ways of improving the orientation process.
- Consider inviting a person's family or significant other for an orientation. You will demonstrate your interest in the total person.

Outdoor Training

More than 100 consultants in North America provide outdoor training experiences to individuals and organizations, attesting to the popularity of this form of training. Working and playing together within a different environment can bring about the following changes:

- *Changed relationships.* People seem more prepared to deal with issues that are otherwise too uncomfortable to address at work, such as differences in workplace values.
- *A changed mind-set.* People might be less reliant on old paradigms and be more willing to change their mind-set.
- *Changed perspective.* Experiencing coworkers in a new setting can lead to opportunities to gain new insight into and appreciation for one another.

- There are two types of outdoor training:
  ✓ Wilderness activities.
  ✓ Outdoor activities in an urban area.
- Wilderness activities can include activities such as these:
  ✓ Hiking
  ✓ Canoeing
  ✓ White-water rafting
  ✓ Rock climbing
- Outdoor activities include:
  ✓ Exercises above ground level, usually using ropes
  ✓ Those that take place at ground level
- These activities can focus on individual achievement or the interaction of people in a team.
- The objectives for outdoor training vary but typically focus on the following:
  ✓ Team building
  ✓ Leadership development
  ✓ Development of self-confidence
  ✓ Problem solving

✓ Decision making
✓ Strengthening loyalty

The Process

- Setting up an outdoor program requires you to identify an issue that cannot easily or effectively be solved by another type of intervention. An example might be poor interpersonal chemistry between two people, loss of enthusiasm, or concerns about the future of the company. If this is the case, seek a consultant who:
  ✓ Has a good track record with similar organizations.
  ✓ Will help customize the program to suit your staff.
  ✓ Can design the program around key objectives.
  ✓ Will provide any necessary follow-up assistance.

The Training

- An effective outdoor program usually follows these steps:
  ✓ Begin with an icebreaker to get people as comfortable with each other as possible.
  ✓ Establish a learning contract, and set any guidelines to ensure health and safety.
  ✓ Take participants on a tour of the site to clear up any misconceptions they may have and increase everyone's comfort level.
  ✓ Conduct warm-up exercises, such as stretching, which will help to prevent injury.
  ✓ Conduct the designed exercises.
  ✓ Debrief, to enable the participants to share their thoughts and receive feedback.
  ✓ Connect the experiences to on-the-job realities.
- To bring closure to a day of challenge and physical exercise, the facilitator should debrief at the conclusion of each day. This review will be more successful if the facilitator-trainer follows these guidelines:
  ✓ Ask the participants if they would welcome feedback.
  ✓ Share all good and negative items, to ensure balance.

✓ Be as specific as possible, supporting the example with a video (if one is available).

✓ Provide every opportunity for the participants to identify their own problems and solutions.

✓ Stick to the facts without being judgmental and citing how you would have handled the situation.

- At the debriefing a good facilitator will:

✓ Maintain some structure but loosen or tighten it as appropriate.

✓ Ensure that participants do not disclose inappropriate information (to the extent that that can be done).

✓ Respect confidentiality, as appropriate.

✓ Monitor that people do not get hurt if they naively disclose information that might otherwise come back to haunt them.

Outsourcing

Organizations everywhere are focusing resources and energy on managing their core businesses and are finding it more economical to outsource some activities to specialists who can demonstrate quality, delivery, and cost competitiveness.

- Organizations outsource a variety of training activities, including these:
    - ✓ Specialized course development
    - ✓ Specialized course delivery
    - ✓ Training needs analysis
    - ✓ Training facilities
    - ✓ Designing information systems that track training statistics
    - ✓ Training administration
- Outsourcing some or all training activities should be considered if any of the following conditions holds for your organization:
    - ✓ Demand for training fluctuates during the year and from year to year.
    - ✓ In-house expertise cannot meet some specialized training requirements.
    - ✓ A specific training need is a one-time only occurrence.
    - ✓ The ongoing costs of an in-house training department become difficult to justify.
    - ✓ There is a high rate of no-shows for your training courses, which can imply that the curriculum is not relevant to the organization's challenges.
    - ✓ Training department staff are often deployed to other functions to meet operational needs.
    - ✓ Your organization is spending significantly more than similar-size organizations for the same amount of training.
- Outsourcing has a number of advantages:
    - ✓ Reduced overhead costs
    - ✓ A direct relationship between training needs and training costs

✓ Meaningful cost-benefit analysis applied to training requirements
✓ Focused expectations for results, based on expenditures
✓ A wider selection of qualified professionals to meet organization needs
✓ The ability to terminate unproductive consulting relationships
✓ Better ability to use the latest methodology and training techniques
✓ Greater competitiveness by using current information
✓ Accurate tracking of training costs
✓ Reduced administrative costs incurred in managing training
✓ Just-in-time delivery for important initiatives
• The disadvantages of outsourcing are these:
    ✓ Typically higher costs for outsourcing on a project-by-project basis
    ✓ The use of consultants who may not understand your business plan
    ✓ The use of consultants who are not as committed to your corporate objectives as in-house training staff may be
    ✓ Confusion generated in your employee population by a multiplicity of messages and biases from consultants
    ✓ Reliance on consultants' availability for scheduling delivery dates
    ✓ No on-site availability of internal training consultants for impromptu meetings about training requirements
    ✓ Time-consuming research about prospective consultants and meetings and interviews with them
    ✓ Training initiatives that may not be linked easily to your organization's recruitment, promotion, and career development strategies
    ✓ Potential breaches of confidentiality with respect to important corporate strategies
• Each organization makes its own decisions about the cost-effectiveness of outsourcing depending on the availability and cost of internal training staff. When outsourcing does occur, the cost-benefit analysis should be reviewed regularly in the light of changing business variables.

Overhead Do's and Don'ts

Using the overhead correctly will add to the effectiveness of your presentation and message. Here are key ideas to help you.

- Check that the light bulb is working. If your machine uses two light bulbs in case one fails, check both.
- Learn how to use the overhead *before* your presentation. Different manufacturers have different switching systems.
- Focus the machine before you start to avoid the embarrassment of an indistinct picture. Make sure the picture is exactly on the screen.
- Clean the face plate to remove dirt that will project on the screen.
- Number your transparencies, and have them laid out in front of you so you can see the next one before you get to it. This will help you to bridge the information from one transparency to the next, thereby knitting your presentation together.
- Use the "four-by-four" rule: Try not to exceed four lines per transparency and more than four words per line.
- Don't use your fingers to point to items on your transparency. Your hand might shake, making people aware of your nervousness. Use a stir stick or pencil (not a round one, which will roll).
- Show all the information first. Then refer to each item one by one.
- Don't block the audience's view of the visuals.
- Your overheads will be effective if you follow these guidelines:
  - ✓ Use bold, capital letters.
  - ✓ Avoid using red: this color is more difficult to read than any other.
  - ✓ Add or change color for headings and bullets.
  - ✓ Emphasize headings by making them larger.
  - ✓ Use only one idea or concept per transparency.

✓ Use diagrams and graphs to increase audience understanding.
✓ Add pictures to create an impression as well as increase
  understanding.
✓ Keep each transparency simple.

Participation in Workshops

A trainer should give everyone the opportunity to get involved, practice skills, and influence both the process and content of the session. Care should be taken to provide the opportunity and encouragement for those not typically vocal.

- There are three types of people who do not participate actively in workshops:
  - ✓ Introverts
  - ✓ Shy people
  - ✓ People who do not want to be in the training

Introverts

- Introverted people do not lack confidence, as may be the case with shy people. They are characterized as:
  - ✓ Wanting to think before they talk.
  - ✓ Having less need to influence the workshop.
  - ✓ Getting internal satisfaction from new ideas, without the need to confirm their satisfaction with others.
- Ways to involve introverts include:
  - ✓ Conducting a round robin. This process gives each person a chance to express an opinion in rotation. Participants can choose to say "pass." Because introverts need to think first, they often give their ideas in the second round of a round robin.
  - ✓ Giving them advanced notice of the topic.
  - ✓ Asking them by name for their suggestions.

Shy People

- Shy people may be unwilling to share their ideas for fear of ridicule.

- Shy people can best be drawn out by using one or a combination of these strategies:
  - ✓ Ask them to give their ideas in writing.
  - ✓ Ask them low-risk questions and thank them for their input. This success will gradually develop their confidence.
  - ✓ Watch and respond to their body language. When they indicate that they are ready to contribute—they typically lean forward and appear ready to talk—invite them to speak.
  - ✓ Initially ask them for low-risk opinions, which could involve a simple yes or no reply.
- Other strategies that will encourage more involvement from quieter trainees include the following:
  - ✓ Never put people down.
  - ✓ Get them to comment on something that you know that they have an interest in, an opinion on, or can do well.
  - ✓ Use more small group activities, as opposed to lecturing.
  - ✓ Avoid theater-style seating. Use tables for five or six participants, or use a U-shaped format.
  - ✓ Pair people up early so they establish a buddy.
  - ✓ Ask trainees to act as the recorder on the flip chart.
  - ✓ Balance your presentation with listening.
  - ✓ Develop trust with people. Sit next to them during exercises, nod agreement when they talk, and engage them in discussion at the breaks.
  - ✓ Project positive body language, and smile often. Lean forward and maintain eye contact when trainees talk to you.
  - ✓ Ask open-ended questions to encourage people to open up.
  - ✓ Get trainees to put their first names on both sides of their tent card so that you and the people around them can address them by name and interact more freely with them.
  - ✓ Delegate tasks as may be appropriate to show your confidence in trainees.
  - ✓ Use a low-risk icebreaker at the beginning of the session to get people comfortable as quickly as possible.

Unwilling Trainees

- One of the greatest challenges for a trainer is involving participants who, for a variety of reasons, do not want to be there at all. This kind of attitude, if not dealt with, can spread rapidly to other trainees.

- Here are some tips for dealing with reluctant trainees:
  - ✓ Speak about the teaching principles with conviction, not with zeal. Conviction is appealing; zeal may be a turn-off.
  - ✓ At the beginning of the session, have each participant describe one practical thing they want to get out of the session.
  - ✓ Invite the group to address any negative comments rather than tackling the matter yourself. If no one responds, simply state that you respect the person's point of view and hope that his or her time will not be wasted.
  - ✓ Always include a number of quizzes or challenges during a course. Few people can resist a chance to "strut their stuff."
  - ✓ Self-assessment exercises or a personal mastery test are often hard to resist. Even if these are done in private (which most should be to avoid embarrassing people) it is an opportunity to get everyone engaged.
  - ✓ Include team exercises in the session. A negative person who may risk embarrassing or sabotaging the trainer is less likely to be seen as uncooperative with a small group of colleagues.

Peer Training

P eer training involves people at the same level in the organization in coaching, training, and mentoring each other—a highly effective form of training.

- Peer training is effective for those situations in which:
  - ✓ You have knowledgeable "expert peers" available to train others.
  - ✓ The subject matter can be broken down into bite-size pieces, for easy consumption.
  - ✓ The in-house subject matter experts are willing and able to train their peers.
  - ✓ The peer experts do not feel threatened by sharing their knowledge.
  - ✓ Information is or can easily be documented.
- Peer training can be used to learn any of the following skills:
  - ✓ Business skills, such as budgeting
  - ✓ Social skills, such as giving feedback
  - ✓ Team skills, such as running effective meetings
  - ✓ Technical skills, such as using a computer
- Peer training is often more effective than training done by an outside "expert," for these reasons:
  - ✓ The content is authentic and believable.
  - ✓ Skepticism is reduced as there is little fear of a hidden agenda.
  - ✓ The cost is low, because the training is done without an outside consultant or facilitator.
  - ✓ There is little time wasted because training is done on the spot, without any need to travel to another venue.
  - ✓ Training is usually put into practice right away, thereby reinforcing the learning experience.
  - ✓ Training is typically done on a just-in-time basis.
- Finding the right person to conduct the training is the key to success. Look for employees who are:
  - ✓ Well respected by peers.

✓ Highly competent in the particular skill set you are looking to train.
✓ Patient.
✓ Good listeners.
✓ Excellent communicators.
✓ Typically upbeat and positive.
✓ Trained to train.
✓ Have an ability to simplify things.

- The most effective type of peer training is that in which people are self-directed and become involved in choosing the following:
  ✓ What they need to learn
  ✓ When they will do it
  ✓ How they will learn
  ✓ Where they will get the resources from
- There are two types of peer training:
  ✓ One-on-one training
  ✓ Training in teams
- On-the-job peer training is most effective if the trainer follows a simple step-by-step process of breaking tasks down into small pieces (modules). Each task is then taught as follows:
  1. Set objectives.
  2. Explain the task.
  3. Demonstrate how it should be done.
  4. Let the trainee try the task.
  5. Provide positive reinforcement if the task is done right; redirect the trainee if a mistake has been made.
- Peer training in a group has similarities to one-on-one coaching, but the process lends itself to learning interpersonal skills, team skills, and the like. An effective peer learning team would use the following agenda in their meeting:
  1. Review the success with which they put previous learning into practice.
  2. Develop and agree on new learning objectives.
  3. Review the theory.
  4. Share personal experiences and case studies.
  5. Practice the new skill.
  6. Give feedback.
  7. Commit to practicing the new skill.
  8. Summarize what has been learned.

Preparing for Training

Proper preparation for training will allow you to present information in a relaxed, effective, and professional manner. This checklist will help you avoid some common pitfalls.

- Book meeting rooms early, advise attendees of the location, and provide maps to it if necessary.
- Confirm the number of attendees.
- Assemble your materials and supporting documentation.
- Confirm your meeting room reservation and ensure that refreshments have been ordered.
- If the presentation is complex, have a package of information prepared for each participant. Distribute these in advance for everyone to review prior to the session.
- Do a dry run to test the materials and your self-confidence. Imagine the audience in front of you. Gauge their reaction. Consider videotaping your practice session so that you can refine it as may be appropriate.
- Review your objectives to make sure they are in line with what you intend to deliver. Better still, make sure that what you intend to deliver is directly related to the objectives.
- Assemble a backup emergency kit of markers, masking tape, name cards, spare bulbs for equipment, pencils, and pens.
- Meet with some attendees beforehand to gauge their enthusiasm for the upcoming presentation or their concerns. If you detect any resistance, give them an opportunity to vent by:
  - ✓ Listening.
  - ✓ Showing empathy.
  - ✓ Offering to address their concern if at all possible.
- Learn as much as you can about the training audience: their skill levels, demographics, and prior training experiences.
- Test-drive the overhead projector, VCR, and room lighting.
- Review the evaluations from other groups to whom you've given the course. Determine which topics generated the least interest or most confusion, and analyze why.
- Talk with the manager or managers of the participants to find

out as much as you can about their learning styles, communication styles, and general enthusiasm about training.

- Get a sense about other organization issues that may be playing on the trainees' minds: downsizing, new performance measures, upcoming management changes, and so forth.
- Develop a workplace profile of the group. Is there some natural tension among participants already (e.g., managers attending along with their direct reports? union and nonunion employees in the group? salaried and paid-by-the-hour employees?)
- Conduct an informal telephone survey with some participants to understand their expectations and previous training experiences, good and bad.
- Call someone who has trained the group before. What are this person's observations?
- Develop a short quiz for trainees to complete (anonymously) before training. Focus on their expectations and their experience in the subject matter.
- Arrive at the session as early as possible to mingle with the group, and get a sense about their enthusiasm for the subject matter.

Presentation Skills

I rrespective of the type of information you need to communicate, you will improve retention by making the transfer interesting, challenging, and fun.

Here's how

- Relax, and welcome people into the meeting room. Show your confidence and approachability with a firm handshake and a smile.
- When everyone is seated, welcome them officially, and let them know what to expect. Remind them of your agenda, the expected outcome, the amount of time you intend to take, and break times. Tell them you will pass out copies of the presentation after you have made it. Also, let them know where the rest rooms and fire exits are.
- Start off with as much impact as possible. Present a challenge or recall a story that will move your audience.
- Ask rhetorical questions from time to time. Challenge your audience. Conduct periodic polls by asking a question that needs a show of hands for an answer.
- When you conduct a question-and-answer session, focus on those people who have demonstrated from the start of the session that they are likely to be constructive and positive.
- Keep the presentation to the point. Don't cover material that the audience already knows. Focus on new information.
- Do not read word for word from your notes, slides, or overheads. The audience can do that too. Give people a chance to read each visual; then paraphrase the content, stressing key points.
- Provide a bridging comment between each overhead or slide to knit your presentation together.
- Keep eye contact with your audience. Also:
    ✓ Scan the audience, looking at each person for three to five seconds if your audience is small.
    ✓ Don't read off the screen or turn your back on the audience.

- Keep people's attention by:
  - ✓ Changing the pace of presentation from time to time.
  - ✓ Doing something different at least every seven minutes (e.g., ask questions, poll the audience, complete questionnaires, do group work).
  - ✓ Modulating your voice, speaking loudly and then softly, quickly and then deliberately.
  - ✓ Animating your facial expressions and gestures.
  - ✓ Gesturing appropriately.
- Move around the room, getting closer to your audience when they ask questions. Staying behind a podium will build a wall between you and your audience.
- Grab the audience's attention:
  - ✓ Challenge your audience by starting off with one of the five Ws and an H.
    - —Who would like . . . ?
    - —What would be the one . . . ?
    - —When was the last time you . . . ?
    - —Where is the best place you . . . ?
    - —Why is it that . . . ?
    - —How can you . . . ?
  - ✓ Quote a shocking statistic, or take a controversial stance.
  - ✓ Start with humor, but only if you are good at telling jokes and only if the story is relevant to the subject. A failed joke will just increase tension and your embarrassment. The best humor is a story that is self-deprecating. Such a story will not only amuse your audience but develop a link with them, since you are signaling to them that you are "normal." Never tell a joke that could offend.
- Use gestures to increase your effectiveness.
  - ✓ Open your arms to the audience, when appropriate, as if to embrace them.
  - ✓ Keep your arms at your sides when you are not using them.
  - ✓ Keep arm gestures between your waist and shoulder.
  - ✓ Avoid quick and jerky gestures, which give the impression of nervousness.
  - ✓ Vary your gestures to suit your message. A continuous single gesture will be distracting.
  - ✓ Don't overuse gestures, or they will lose their impact.

- Use as much of the space in front of your audience as possible. Avoid standing behind a lectern.
- Involve your audience; for instance, take a poll, ask for opinions, or find out if anyone can relate to the example you have described. This interaction will show you are interested in and care about the opinion of your audience.
- Improve retention and interest:
  - ✓ Share anecdotes that illustrate key points. People will visualize the story and remember it.
  - ✓ Use analogies—for example, "Working without goals is like traveling without a map."
  - ✓ Use metaphors. Saying, "That salesperson is like a fox" is more effective than saying, "He is clever."
- Use props to add impact. Hold up articles, books, or magazines when you quote from recognized experts.
- Use your voice to add impact.
  - ✓ Change you voice modulation. Speak quickly or slowly, loudly or softly, for brief periods.
  - ✓ Generally speak a little louder than you do normally.
  - ✓ Pause before or after a key thought.
  - ✓ If you are not sure what to say, pause briefly to collect your thoughts, but *without saying "um" or "ah."*
- Project positive body language, which will convey your confidence to the audience.
  - ✓ Stand erect and tall, and push your chest out.
  - ✓ Avoid putting your hands on one or both hips, a stance that projects arrogance.
  - ✓ A protrusion of one hip signals that you don't want to be there. So does a prolonged eye blink.
  - ✓ Maintain steady eye contact with your audience. Fast-shifting eyes indicate a lack of certainty.
- End with a challenge that leaves the audience with something to think about.

Product Training

Product training, a core ingredient of most corporate training agendas, may be directed to an organization's employees or its customers.

The need to conduct product training is usually ongoing, because:

- New products are introduced frequently.
- Products are changed frequently.
- Employees are hired or promoted to positions requiring product marketing or product sales.
- Product pricing structures change.
- Internal processes that have an impact on requisitioning and product delivery change significantly over time.

Here are some important guidelines for designing and delivering product training.

Content

- Always include lessons that identify a product's features (its characteristics) and its benefits (how it helps the customer).
- Include information about your organization's big picture in selling the product: intended market penetration, sales volumes, revenues, and profits, for example.
- Describe and discuss any competitors' products.
- Present and discuss customer research, including feedback from focus groups, test marketing, and customer satisfaction studies.
- Develop clear guidelines for all internal processes that have an impact on selling or marketing the product: requisitioning, approval processes, and delivery arrangements.

Materials

- Secure all materials in easy-to-use binders that allow participants to add updates about features and processes.
- Divide the binder into easy reference components: pricing, benefits, marketplace analysis, and so forth.
- Distribute customer brochures and any other information that has been circulated publicly about the product, including news releases.
- Prepare a one-page summary with names and contact details for managers or specialists who can provide further information or hot-line assistance.
- Design a chart that demonstrates the process flow as the product moves from the design stage through to customer delivery.
- Use pictures and charts to support teaching principles and examples whenever practical.
- Prepare a question-and-answer sheet that anticipates customer concerns.

Delivery

- Whenever possible, have samples of the product or a computer simulation for hands-on practice or demonstration.
- Use a ratio of three-to-one for discussion and practice versus lecture.
- Include realistic role plays as part of the practice. Use information from experienced sales and marketing staff for the role plays.
- Use short quizzes to gauge the audience's understanding after each short subject.
- Product training can be dry. Include a video that demonstrates sales, marketing, or listening skills to relieve the emphasis on specific product information.
- Keep an ongoing record of unexpected questions and concerns. Commit to a quick response to them.
- Be realistic about the course length. Don't cram too much information into a day. On the other hand, short modules over a period of time might compromise the course's impact and momentum.

- Solicit realistic input from participants about potential barriers to selling or marketing the product. Remember that equipping people to market or sell a product is not the same as motivating them to sell or market.

Professional Associations: A Checklist for Selecting and Joining

Professional associations keep trainers abreast of trends and help to develop contacts for sharing information. The number of associations is increasing as new training specializations emerge (e.g., multimedia).

- The primary benefits of joining an association are:
  - ✓ Networking opportunities
  - ✓ Professional development
  - ✓ Access to up-to-date research
- Here are some guidelines and important questions in deciding which association(s) to join, especially if affordability is an issue. Talk to employees of the association itself, as well as with your professional colleagues, and establish the following:
  - ✓ Does membership entitle you to reduced conference fees? Are the discounts significant?
  - ✓ Does the association publish an annual member directory? This is an important networking tool.
  - ✓ Is there a local chapter in your area?
  - ✓ Does the local chapter meet regularly, and if so how often?
  - ✓ Do your professional colleagues recommend the association?
  - ✓ Does the association publish a regular newsletter or magazine?
  - ✓ Is the information the association provides relevant and interesting?
  - ✓ Is association information accessible on the Internet?
  - ✓ Does the association provide specialized research on request, e.g., "best practices," statistics, case studies?
  - ✓ Has the membership base increased annually?

- ✓ What percentage of members renew their membership annually?
- ✓ Are participant evaluation summaries available from previous conferences and seminars?
- ✓ Who is the executive director of the association, and what are his or her credentials?
- ✓ Who are the board members of the association?
- ✓ What is the profile of the membership base: their experience levels, industry groups, and so forth?
- ✓ Does the association set professional standards that are recognized in the industry?
- ✓ Does the association conduct certification programs that are recognized in the industry?
- ✓ Are you treated with courtesy when you call in person or on the phone?
- ✓ Is there a resource center at the association office that members can use?
- ✓ Does membership entitle you to discounts on training videos and books?
- ✓ How does the cost of membership compare with other professional associations?
- Your decision about joining a particular association will be based on your own specific professional development interests.
- To reduce costs and maximize your opportunity to take advantage of multiple memberships, consider:
  - ✓ Sharing a membership with others in your company.
  - ✓ Exchanging association literature with colleagues who have joined other associations.
  - ✓ Using the Internet for information and advice.
- Finally, if dollars are tight, consider forming an informal networking group. Assign research projects to members, exchange interesting articles, and share experiences.

Record Keeping

Organizations large and small face a common challenge in maintaining training records that are both useful and up-to-date.

Whether records are kept in sophisticated computer databases or on index cards, there are three fundamental issues:

1. What to keep
2. Why to keep them
3. How to keep them

What Records to Keep

- At a minimum, your records should contain:
  - ✓ Internal course participant lists for each course by date and location (don't worry about aggregating the list; you can always create a master list if you want or need one).
  - ✓ Confirmed registrations for upcoming courses, by date and location.
  - ✓ Waiting lists for upcoming courses.
  - ✓ Registration for self-service training packages and programs.
  - ✓ Evaluation summaries for each course, by date and location (restrict the information to two or three key effectiveness indicators).
  - ✓ Cost of each course, by date and location.
- Some companies opt to keep additional information on file. Bear in mind, however, that the more information you keep, the greater the likelihood is that your system may get backlogged in information entry. This optional information can include:
  - ✓ External courses attended by employees.
  - ✓ Courses completed under the tuition-reimbursement program.

✓ Professional development conferences and seminars attended by employees.
✓ Books and videos on loan from employee resource centers.

Why to Keep Records

- The most common uses for a training record-keeping system are:
  ✓ A composite organization profile of skill training.
  ✓ A statistical database about annual training costs and total training days.
  ✓ A tool for selecting and scheduling upcoming courses.
  ✓ A user-friendly course registration system.
  ✓ A user-friendly registration cancellation system.
  ✓ A list of candidates who are available on short notice to take advantage of canceled registrations.
  ✓ A budgeting and invoicing tool if training costs are charged back to functional units.
  ✓ Information that can complement human resources data about the relationship of skills training to employee promotions and reassignments.
  ✓ Utilization rates for self-study tools.
  ✓ A guide for identifying potential executive succession candidates, as well as coaches, mentors, or tutors.
  ✓ Training statistics about target groups that are fundamental to the success of affirmative action or employment equity initiatives.

How to Keep Records

- Restrict employee data to names and positions only. If you need to undertake a sophisticated analysis, you can reconstruct any other information as required.
- If your internal human resources information system is cumbersome or out of date, there are several low-cost, effective, software packages on the market.
- Have course participants fill out a master registration sheet at the start of the session; use this as your input document, and

keep it on file. This avoids the issue of no-shows or extras that
advance registration can't report.

- Retain course lists for no more than two years. Any older information is usually irrelevant because of changes to course
  content and employee turnover.
- Retain advance registration requests for six months.
- Retain waiting lists for three months.
- Do not attempt to maintain individual employee profiles. That
  is the responsibility of employees and their managers.
- Exhibit 8 is a straightforward course record that can be kept
  manually or electronically for every session. The information
  from all courses can be easily compiled on a monthly or annual basis to give you a quick snapshot of your overall training investment.

Exhibit 8. Course record.

Course Name: Advanced Management
HELD AT: Chicago *DATE:* May 1–3/98

Participants/Title:

Summary

Total participants   = 20
Course length   = 3 days
Total training days = 60
Total cost   = $6,000

Evaluation Summary (scale of 1–7)

Course effectiveness   = 5/7
Facilitator effectiveness = 6/7

Requests for Proposal

Many companies use requests for proposal (RFPs) when contracting training services. These are formal documents that set out criteria and specifications for training projects. Companies may invite selected vendors to bid for the project or publicize the RFP in an open forum, such as a trade journal.

- The advantages of using an RFP for training services are:
  - ✓ Expectations for the project are clear.
  - ✓ Proposals from vendors are in a consistent format.
  - ✓ Decision making is enhanced by comparing vendors against common criteria.
- RFPs are most commonly used for the following reasons:
  - ✓ The project is extensive in terms of size, budget, and impact.
  - ✓ A company's administrative procedures stipulate that all contracts over a set price must be put to bid.
  - ✓ A number of people will be involved in the decision.
  - ✓ The decision makers do not have in-depth knowledge of the products and services available in the marketplace.
  - ✓ It is anticipated that it will be difficult to choose among many competent vendors.
  - ✓ It is in the company's best interest to be perceived as fair and equitable in awarding contracts.
- RFPs can include as many criteria as deemed important. As a minimum, all RFPs should include:
  - ✓ A clear description of the project and anticipated outcomes.
  - ✓ The number of employees to be trained.
  - ✓ Deadline date for the receipt of a completed RFP.
  - ✓ Deadline date for the completion of the project.
- State your expectations or have vendors make recommendations for these criteria:
  - ✓ Pricing.
  - ✓ Key teaching principles.
  - ✓ Project evaluation criteria.
  - ✓ Meetings with the company.

- ✓ Materials (e.g., workbooks, handouts).
- ✓ Invoicing and payment guidelines.
- Additional vendor information in the completed RFP can help the decision-making process:
  - ✓ Company background.
  - ✓ Financial statements.
  - ✓ Facilitator profiles.
  - ✓ Client profiles and references.
  - ✓ Professional accreditation.
  - ✓ Sample materials, such as workbooks.
- Sometimes special circumstances should be noted in the RFP—for example:
  - ✓ A requirement to conduct training and develop materials in a second language, such as French or Spanish.
  - ✓ Potential conflict of interest (some companies require vendors to declare any family relationships in the company).
  - ✓ A requirement for potential vendors to declare current or recent contracts with competitors.
- In choosing a format for your RFP, consider these options:
  - ✓ A standard form already used by your company for awarding contracts.
  - ✓ An adaptation of a form used by your company.
  - ✓ An adaptation of a form developed for training contracts used by other companies.
- The time, research, and energy that vendors invest in responding to RFPs can be extensive. Some companies pay a small fee to vendors for completed proposals as an acknowledgment of the investment. Although not common, this practice demonstrates your commitment to effective decision making based on comprehensive information.
- Here are some guidelines for consultants who are responding to an organization's request for proposal:
  - ✓ Use your network to discover as much as you can about the organization's culture: its employee population, its market challenges, its training priorities, and which consulting organizations have worked with the company in the past.
  - ✓ Make sure that your proposal addresses the specific training need outlined in the proposal; do not use the proposal as an introduction to your full complement of services or to sell a more comprehensive training solution.

✓ If you include references, make sure they are specific about whom to contact in the organization, his or her title, and when the project was done.

✓ Invest in high quality stationery and binders for your proposal.

✓ If you fax your proposal, follow up with a hard copy by mail or courier.

✓ Beware presumptuous statements in your cover letter or introduction ("I am sure you want to be the top service provider . . ."). You should, however, refer to information the organization provided, such as a mission statement, and demonstrate how your proposal can support it.

Resistance to Training

Before you can teach people anything, you may have to overcome their resistance; otherwise you will feel as if you are pushing a rope. Here are the main sources of resistance and some useful strategies to counter them.

Source 1: Group Resistance

- Cooperating with the trainer might be viewed as being a traitor if the objectives of the training appear contrary to the interests of the group. A teamwork program, for example, might be seen as a productivity enhancement program that would cause layoffs. In the event that participants are ganging up against you, you should:
  ✓ Not avoid the issue but rather tackle it head-on.
  ✓ Deal with it whenever you feel no meeting of the minds.
  ✓ Not single anyone out.
  ✓ Point out your observations and feelings, and ask for confirmation that there is a problem.
  ✓ Show your interest by listening and not being defensive.
  ✓ Engage the group in finding ways to deal with the problem.
  ✓ Separate issues that can be dealt with inside the workshop with those that can only be fixed outside (if at all). Deal with matters that can be fixed and over which people in the workshop have control. Also, ask people to take responsibility for the other issues outside the session at a later time.

Source 2: Resistance to Change

- People who have been working in certain ways for years may find it difficult to accept radically different approaches. Try these strategies:

✓ Encourage them to make smaller changes.
✓ Have them practice new skills without any chance of losing face or being ridiculed.
✓ Find the cause of the resistance and encourage discussion of it.
✓ Demonstrate the new behavior or skill yourself, and get feedback about positive impacts
✓ Canvass the opinions of those who are in favor of the change
✓ Provide rewards for changed behavior, no matter how slight.
✓ Empathize with people's unwillingness to try to change.

Source 3: Fear of Appearing Foolish

- Doing something wrong in front of others might cause embarrassment. A person might refuse to experiment rather than seem incompetent. Some strategies to adopt include these:
  ✓ Develop an understanding up-front about people's needing to take risks.
  ✓ Do not permit ridicule.
  ✓ Laugh at your own mistakes if they occur.
  ✓ Keep the session light with lots of humor to create a relaxed, more permissive environment.

Source 4: Unclear Goals and Objectives

- Often people are sent to a workshop with inaccurate or no information about the course objectives. They may become openly hostile if they find themselves hostage to something they have limited use for, or they may become withdrawn and uncooperative, taxing the patience of all those in the room.
  ✓ Don't confront them in the class. You do not need a standoff that will produce a win-lose or lose-lose outcome. Speak to them at the first break. Empathize with their frustration, and ask them for help with a solution.
  ✓ Offer to help with their issues by adding *their* learning

needs to the agenda or giving them an opportunity to share their experiences and knowledge with others.

✓ If their needs cannot be met during the session, offer to help later.

✓ If you feel that your objectives and those of most of the trainees are not in synch, renegotiate the learning objectives, and do your best to modify the program. If this is difficult, at least give people a chance to vent, and listen with empathy.

✓ If the program is mandatory, consider shortening it in return for participants' cooperation.

Resource Centers

Many companies provide resource centers that give employees access to self-instruction books and videos, training information, and reference materials to encourage individual career management.

- Whether the center is large or small, it must meet these standards to attract employees:
  - ✓ Convenient location
  - ✓ Well organized
  - ✓ Up-to-date and relevant information
  - ✓ Pleasant ambiance
- When planning a center, your feasibility analysis should include these elements:
  - ✓ Formal and informal employee feedback about the kinds of information and tools they want
  - ✓ Space considerations (e.g., shelving, desks, reception area, seminar rooms)
  - ✓ Electrical outlets for telephones, computer systems, and VCRs
  - ✓ Availability of paid staff or volunteers to provide information, update material, and keep records
  - ✓ After-hours access and security
  - ✓ Start-up costs (furniture, equipment, moving costs)
  - ✓ Annual materials costs (for books, videos, subscriptions to professional journals, and catalogs)
- Determine what kinds of record keeping and tracking the center will require, such as:
  - ✓ Employee visits
  - ✓ Loaning out materials
  - ✓ Seminar presentations
  - ✓ Employee success stories
- Budgets vary considerably from company to company. As a minimum standard, all centers should stock:
  - ✓ In-house training catalogs, training course updates, and registration procedures

- ✓ Brochures about external courses
- ✓ Catalogs from local colleges and universities
- ✓ Company annual reports
- ✓ Company organization charts
- ✓ A selection of useful trade and industry journals
- ✓ Recommended reading lists for key management and technical topics
- ✓ A selection of topical books and videos
- ✓ Newspaper clippings about the company
- ✓ Sample workbooks used in popular in-house courses
- Standard equipment in resource centers should include:
  - ✓ Telephones
  - ✓ Computer terminals (with Internet access)
  - ✓ VCRs
  - ✓ Photocopy machine
  - ✓ Bulletin board
  - ✓ Fax machine
- Here are some suggestions for gathering interesting and up-to-date materials:
  - ✓ Many managers regularly receive promotional books and videos. Ask them to donate these materials to the center after reviewing them.
  - ✓ Many newspapers review topical business books. Keep these reviews on file.
  - ✓ Ask employees who attend external courses to prepare a short summary about the course for retention in the center.
  - ✓ Set up a partnership with local libraries for lending new business books and videos.
  - ✓ Once a year, ask all employees to go through their offices and send interesting books and articles they have accumulated to the center.
  - ✓ Videotape key presentations by the executive team members for viewing.
  - ✓ Visit other resource centers to check out the materials they have.
  - ✓ Offer to do book reviews in exchange for a free copy.
  - ✓ Ask consultants that the company uses regularly to donate materials and workbooks.
- It is difficult to keep materials organized and up-to-date. Here are some suggestions for keeping clutter under control:

- ✓ Ask for staff volunteers in exchange for certain privileges such as borrowing videotapes or free tickets to seminars.
- ✓ Use students and interns from local colleges or universities to organize the center.
- ✓ Retain as much material as possible in three-ring binders.
- ✓ Keep circulars and articles for six months only.
- ✓ Sort through catalogs annually.
- ✓ Laminate important handouts.
- To generate interest in using the center, consider these suggestions:
  - ✓ Invite employees to give short talks about areas of specialization.
  - ✓ Set up cross-functional panels to talk about current company challenges.
  - ✓ Invite consultants to give free "lunch-and-learn" seminars as a way of marketing their services.
  - ✓ Use the bulletin board to list employees who are willing to tutor, coach, or mentor other employees.
  - ✓ Keep records of course evaluations for employees to review.

Rewards and Recognition

S uccessful organizations do not merely *record* training results; they *celebrate* learning opportunities and outcomes.
Coaches and trainers have the ability to influence the learning
process by how, when, and where they recognize and reward
learners. Here are some guidelines.

- Celebrating training results has three important benefits to an
  organization:
  - ✓ Demonstrates the commitment of the executive team to en-
    hancing productivity through training
  - ✓ Acknowledges the time and energy that employees invest
    in learning
  - ✓ Reinforces the importance of learning as a strategy for suc-
    cess
- Ideally, the organization should recognize people:
  - ✓ Soon after they have achieved a learning objective.
  - ✓ By being specific as to their accomplishment.
  - ✓ By challenging them with the next goal.
- Recognition can be done:
  - ✓ In front of peers.
  - ✓ In private.
- Recognition and rewards should target the individual learn-
  er's ability.
  - ✓ People who find learning a challenge should be rewarded
    for their effort and some accomplishment.
  - ✓ Average learners should be rewarded for achieving agreed-
    on goals.
  - ✓ The most highly motivated and successful learners should
    be rewarded for exceeding learning goals.
- The choice of where to recognize people should be influenced
  by how the learning goal was set.
  - ✓ If the learning goal was set between the trainer and trainee
    in private, the recognition can be one-on-one.

✓ If the goal was set in a classroom, it would be appropriate to provide accolades in the group setting.

- There are many ways to reward and recognize organization training achievements:

    ✓ Post graphs or charts that track one or two key measures that are affected by training. Update the graphs monthly.

    ✓ Issue certificates for completed courses. Mail the certificates to each employee's home to encourage discussion about the key learning principles with his or her family.

    ✓ Issue certificates for successful completion of self-study courses.

    ✓ Post lists of course participants in an employee resource center. Use this list to identify potential coaches and tutors.

    ✓ Take group photographs at the end of courses, and create a corporate gallery in a high-traffic area.

    ✓ Include action shots taken during training courses in annual reports and company newsletters.

    ✓ Benchmark your training practices against your competitors' or industry standards, and circulate the information to all levels in the organization.

    ✓ Invite recent participants from a course to teach selected modules at the next scheduled course presentation.

    ✓ Solicit testimonials from course participants to use in course catalogs.

    ✓ Develop one-page summaries of content and key learning outcomes for each course offered, and issue special three-ring binders so that employees can retain and update the information easily.

    ✓ Develop bibliographies for courses. Encourage employees to add to the list (be sure to credit the contributor).

    ✓ Involve employees in focus groups to recommend changes or refinements to course material and content.

    ✓ Establish a "Coach of the Year" award. Have employees nominate managers who have been particularly effective in referring employees to training and doing follow-up after courses.

    ✓ Let course participants choose among themselves who has been the most helpful in contributing to the group learning during a course. Use topical business books for rewards.

    ✓ Let managers know which participants have been particularly attentive or effective in training sessions.

✓ Expand performance evaluations to include information about courses attended and self-study tools utilized during the evaluation period.

✓ Include information about training priorities and practices in orientation programs.

✓ Reward "training-friendly" managers with tickets to specialized seminars or conferences.

✓ Produce an annual video in which the executive team discusses training challenges and successes.

✓ Include information and statistics about training outcomes in the annual report.

✓ Develop a short mission statement about learning for the organization, and include the statement in internal and external communiques.

✓ Give out "dinner for two" certificates to participants who attended lengthy courses, out-of-town courses, or courses that were held outside normal business hours.

✓ Involve employees in developing realistic case studies for courses.

✓ Solicit volunteers to test new or proposed self-study programs. Include their reports in newsletters or other organization updates.

✓ Interview senior managers to determine the formal and informal training they undertook in the past year. Prepare and circulate a summary report that reinforces the link between learning and success.

✓ Some ways of celebrating success in the classroom include:
—Describing your observations to the class and asking them to applaud.
—Applauding when everyone is observing the performance together.
—Giving out token gifts such as candy for a clever comment, a flashlight for a comment that brought clarity to a confused situation, certificates, or gestures, such as a pat on the back or a thumbs-up sign.

✓ Among the least effective recognition is the type that:
—May appear childish.
—Is obtained with little effort.
—Is earned by everyone, even those who made little effort.

—Appears arbitrary, such as the "Trainee of the Month" award.

—Is awarded by committees long after the event.

✓ In all cases, the recognition should match the achievement. The more personal the recognition is, the more effective it will be.

Role-Play: Design and Conduct

Role plays are useful in assisting adults to apply new concepts and skills and in shifting attitudes. This method of experience-based learning reinforces classroom theory.

Clarity of learning outcomes is essential here. Facilitators need to be able to articulate why they want to use a role play and what they hope to accomplish.

- Benefits of role plays:
  - ✓ Reinforcing the classroom theory
  - ✓ Allowing adults to practice new skills in a nonthreatening atmosphere
  - ✓ Feedback from peers
  - ✓ Opportunity to experience how others feel
- *Caution*: Adults do not like to feel incompetent or embarrassed. Design role plays with this in mind.
- Role plays should be designed so that:
  - ✓ The outcomes are clear.
  - ✓ The steps in the process and time lines are laid out.
  - ✓ People play themselves or a particular role or style.
  - ✓ There is, if possible, an opportunity for participants to practice new behavior as a result of the feedback.
- Role plays work best when:
  - ✓ The scenarios are realistic.
  - ✓ There is adequate time to debrief the process.
  - ✓ The role play is followed by theory to reinforce the learning.
- *Cautions*
  - ✓ Never skip the debriefing process. Participants need time to come out of role by talking about how they feel and describing what happened.
  - ✓ If there is not adequate time to debrief the process right after the role play, skip the activity altogether.
- Role plays can occur in pairs, trios, or a group.

Role Plays for Pairs or Trios

- Review the learning outcomes, the steps in the process, and the time available.
  - ✓ Ask people to work in pairs or trios.
  - ✓ Participants choose who will have the major role in demonstrating the skill being learned.
  - ✓ Designate a third person to act as an observer.
  - ✓ Provide observation sheets and guidelines for the observer.
  - ✓ Provide feedback sheets to assist the observer in giving feedback.
  - ✓ Allow preparation time if needed to study the role or relevant information.
  - ✓ The facilitator's role is to observe the groups but not intervene unless participants are off-track or step out of role.
  - ✓ Call time at the end of the first role play.
  - ✓ Allow time for debriefing—feedback from either the receiver or the observer.
  - ✓ Have participants switch roles.
  - ✓ Each member of the pair or trio should have the opportunity to be the giver or initiator.
  - ✓ Repeat this process.
  - ✓ When the pairs or trios have completed the role play, allow for large group discussion of what people learned.

Role Plays in Groups

- Within a group setting, each individual plays an assigned role in accomplishing a particular task. This type of role play can be used to demonstrate:
  - ✓ Teamwork
  - ✓ Meetings
  - ✓ Leadership styles
  - ✓ Conflict resolution
- When particular roles are assigned to individuals:
  - ✓ Hand out copies of each of the roles to each person.
  - ✓ Emphasize that the details supplied for each role are confidential.

- ✓ Allow time for preparation for the role play.
- ✓ Explain that team members cannot reveal to other members their particular role until the role is over.
- Steps for group role plays:
  - ✓ Review the learning outcomes, the steps in the process, and the time available.
  - ✓ Allow preparation time.
  - ✓ The facilitator's role is to observe the group's process but not intervene unless people have misunderstood the instructions or are out of role.
  - ✓ Call time at the end.
  - ✓ Facilitate the debriefing of the process:
    —How do people feel after the role play?
    —What happened?
    —Why did that happen?
    —How might that have been handled differently?
    —Who had control of the discussion?
    —Did anyone feel left out?
  - ✓ Add some of your own observations and ask for explanations and comments from the group.
  - ✓ Encourage everyone to speak.
  - ✓ Allow participants to explain the role they were playing.
  - ✓ Reinforce the learning points with relevant theory.
- An oral debriefing can be followed by a formal team critique, where team members use scaled items to assess how they worked together.

Self-Directed Learning

We can only have citizens who can live construc-
tively in the kaleidoscopically changing world . . . if
we are willing for them to become self-starting, self-
initiating learners.

CARL ROGERS, *Freedom to Learn*

Self-directed learning is the degree to which people are willing and able to take responsibility to learn on their own.
Ideally this implies that the learners:

- Take the initiative to learn.
- Diagnose their own needs.
- Set learning goals.
- Find the resources.
- Pick the method of learning that most appeals to them.
- Implement the learning.
- Evaluate the outcome.

- No organization has unlimited funds to train and develop
  staff. But the training funds can be stretched dramatically if
  an increasing number of people become obliged to upgrade
  their skills on their own.
- Knowledge and skills can be acquired independently in a
  number of ways:
  ✓ Books
  ✓ Self-study programs on tape (audio disk)
  ✓ Videos
  ✓ Self-paced textbooks
  ✓ Computer-based training
  ✓ Interactive video

- ✓ Internet-accessed materials
- ✓ Mentors
- ✓ Coworkers
- ✓ Magazine and journal articles
- ✓ Observation
- ✓ On-site courses
- ✓ Workshops and seminars
- The advantages of self-directed learning are:
  - ✓ The learner has control over pace.
  - ✓ Ownership is high.
  - ✓ Costs are low.
  - ✓ The learner can customize the content.
  - ✓ Training can take place during slow periods of the day.
- Some disadvantages of self-directed learning are:
  - ✓ Most contain generic materials; some parts may be inappropriate for the learner.
  - ✓ Written materials usually can be used only once and cannot be duplicated without breaking copyright laws.
  - ✓ It is difficult to learn managerial skills by any method other than experiential. An understanding of materials may not lead to effective application.
  - ✓ The rate of dropout of self-directed programs is higher than that facilitated by a trained instructor.
- Strategies to evaluate packaged programs include:
  - ✓ Comparing the documented objective against your own.
  - ✓ Checking with others who have used the materials. (Be cautious of this information. Consultants are unlikely to supply the names of unhappy customers.)
  - ✓ Checking with your own network of trainers.
  - ✓ An estimation of the shelf-life of the materials. The longer you can use them without a major update, the more cost-effective they become. Technical subjects date a lot quicker than managerial topics.
  - ✓ Calculating and comparing the cost per trainee for each program.
- The following guidelines are important in self-directed learning programs:
  - ✓ Ensure that materials, such as workbooks and computers, are always available.

✓ Make coaches available for those who need encouragement, guidance, and redirection if they hit a roadblock.

✓ Provide opportunities for people to check their knowledge through self-scoring systems or tests that can be checked by an expert.

✓ Check that the majority of people reach their objective.

✓ If course learning objectives are not being met by most people, investigate the cause.

✓ If dropout rates begin to rise, find out the reason, and fix the problem.

✓ Regularly update materials to ensure that they are easy to follow and error free.

✓ Pilot-test new programs to remove bugs.

✓ Regularly revise course content to ensure that:
   —It relates to actual organization practices (this will enhance credibility and improve the chances of application of skills).
   —It is practical.
   —It is relevant.

✓ Regularly revise program offerings so that you maintain a focus on areas that are a priority with senior management. This will avoid learning for learning's sake.

✓ Self-directed learning is enhanced if the learner commits to a written plan. It will "force" them to:
   —Develop clear learning objectives.
   —Identify actions that will lead to the achievement of those objectives.
   —Set completion dates.
   —Decide how they will know in measurable terms when they are done.

An example of a format for this plan can be found in Exhibit 9.

Exibit 9. Self-directed learning plan.

My Learning Objectives	The Steps I Intend to Take	Target Date	Evaluation Method

Simulations

A simulation is a lifelike enactment, in a classroom-type setting, of the realities of the job. It tests people's ability to apply learning principles.

- Simulations can be used in two situations:
  - ✓ Training
  - ✓ As part of assessing prospective employees
- In training, simulations encourage participants to demonstrate their use of newly acquired skills.
- Assessment centers have become increasingly popular, particularly in companies that are hiring a number of people simultaneously. Simulations enable trained observers to see how people:
  - ✓ Respond under pressure.
  - ✓ Work in a team environment.
  - ✓ Manage priorities.
- Adults enjoy simulations because it gives them a chance to:
  - ✓ Practice a skill.
  - ✓ Get positive feedback.
  - ✓ Build the confidence to use the skill.
  - ✓ Confirm that they understand the theory being taught.
- Simulations can take the form of:
  - ✓ Role plays
  - ✓ Games
  - ✓ Dramatizations of real situations
- The advantages of a simulation are these:
  - ✓ People can practice skills in a nonthreatening environment.
  - ✓ They can make mistakes off rather than on the job.
- Simulations work best when the following principles are followed:
  - ✓ The simulation is done right after a key teaching lesson.
  - ✓ The exercise is realistic; there is no need to stretch the imagination to discover how it might apply in the workplace.
  - ✓ The time allowed does not go beyond what is needed to learn the key principles.

- ✓ Sufficient time is available to debrief and provide feedback to participants. The debriefing should cover what was done well and what might have been done differently.
- ✓ The exercises' complexity is geared to the skill levels of the participants.
- ✓ The exercise should have clearly defined objectives.
- Key design features of successful simulations include:
  - ✓ Having the feeling of being a real situation that has either just happened or is about to happen
  - ✓ Allowing the participants to exceed a satisfactory outcome. This will increase confidence.
  - ✓ Detailed instructions, oral and written.
  - ✓ A flexible design that allows people to customize the details to make it fit better with their world.
  - ✓ The possibility of failure, to allow for learning as a result of the simulation.
  - ✓ Sufficient time for people to regroup and correct their mistakes.
  - ✓ Sufficient time to make it real, but not too long that it drags and leads to boredom.
  - ✓ Checklists that allow participants to record their observations about the use and frequency of the newly acquired skill.

Successful Training Criteria: The Top Ten

The cost of training is high. The payback will increase greatly if one bears in mind these simple principles.

1. *Link all training to the goals of the organization*
   The organization's documented mission should be referred to at the beginning of all training and reviewed at the end to ensure that the skills learned will enable the trainee to make a direct contribution to the overall organization goal.
2. *Get executive-level commitment and involvement*
   Line managers provide the rewards and punishments that send signals about what is important and what is not. They can demonstrate their commitment by:
   ✓ Introducing training sessions.
   ✓ Being available for questions at the end of a session.
   ✓ Following up with participants to ensure that they are putting new skills into practice.
   ✓ Taking courses together with their staff.
   ✓ Rewarding people who are putting new techniques into practice.
   ✓ Using the skills themselves.
   ✓ Specifying skills in people's objectives, to be included in periodic reviews.
3. *Train a critical mass of people*
   The more important a training course is, the more that people need to be involved. Putting the majority of employees through a program sends a strong message about the importance of the program. If the majority of those who attended begin to put the core principles into practice, the culture of the organization will begin to change.
4. *Measure and evaluate results*
   All expenditures should provide a payback, and training programs need to demonstrate a value to the organization by being evaluated. Measurement invariably will lead

to improved performance as results are analyzed and opportunities for improvement are uncovered.

5. *Maintain a customer focus*

No department can operate in a vacuum. Unless the needs of clients are met consistently, the reputation of a training program will deteriorate and program attendance will drop. Internal clients expect their needs to be dealt with quickly and professionally. If costs for programs are charged back to them, they will expect these costs to be competitive.

6. *Use leading-edge adult training practices*

Adults want to be treated as equals by the instructor. They will value training in which they have a good deal of control, are consulted about process and content, work in a safe environment, and have the opportunity to enjoy themselves.

7. *Use the best resources*

As part of the commitment to making training effective, managers need to use the most effective resources available. Sometimes these are available internally, but often they need to be provided by an outside specialist. There is no point in delivering something home-grown if its entire credibility is put into jeopardy because of poor-quality delivery.

8. *Focus on real-world training*

For training to be effective, it needs to be practical and relate to the challenges of the environment to which people will return. Training must go beyond developing awareness and insight, to helping people improve their daily performance.

9. *Operate within the values of the organization*

The values of the organization must be practiced by those providing the training. Showing respect for people, treating all people equally, being prepared, listening, treating people as adults, and striving for excellence are common values that, if made to take a back seat, will guarantee failure.

10. *Involve the target training groups and managers in the program design*

Getting a sample of the audience involved before the workshop will ensure that there is:

✓ Agreement to the content.
✓ Enthusiasm for the program.
✓ Some shared ownership to ensure a successful outcome.

Succession Planning

E ffective succession planning is critical for any organization to ensure little disruption as a result of resignations, transfers, or promotions. There are seven important steps in creating effective succession:

1. Identify the key corporate positions that are fundamental to the organization's success.
2. Nominate high-performing individuals as potential successors. This is often done through succession planning committees with senior representatives of line functions, human resources staff, and training professionals.
3. Assess key gaps in successors' skills to meet current and future requirements.
4. Develop a comprehensive training strategy for successors that encompasses both formal and informal training.
5. Identify and evaluate the training courses and options available that best suit your specific requirements.
6. Calculate the costs of succession training, and create a budget.
7. Implement the succession training plan by identifying key steps, deadlines, and measurement criteria.

Here we look at steps 3 through 7.

Assessing Key Gaps in Successors' Skills

- Interview incumbents of key corporate positions to understand:
  - ✓ Their background and training
  - ✓ Their assessment of future skill requirements
  - ✓ The timeliness of developing effective successors

✓ Their recommendations for effective successor training
✓ Their availability to act as coaches and mentors to successors
✓ Their assessment of successors' strengths and weaknesses
- Interview identified successors to understand their:
  ✓ Training and experience
  ✓ Self-assessment of skills needed in a more senior job
  ✓ Availability for long-term training
  ✓ Recommendations for effective succession training
  ✓ Short-term professional development plans

Developing a Comprehensive Training Strategy

- Identify skills gaps under the headings of:
  ✓ Business skills
  ✓ Industry-specific skills
  ✓ Management skills
- Prioritize the importance of the skill gaps.
- Secure agreement with incumbents and successors about time frames to address skill gaps.
- Determine the best training vehicle to meet skill gaps—for example:
  ✓ Formal training
  ✓ On-the-job training
  ✓ Internal courses
  ✓ External courses
  ✓ Professional upgrading
  ✓ Job rotation
  ✓ Job shadowing
  ✓ Computer-based training
  ✓ Subscriptions to professional journals
  ✓ Task assignment to task forces
  ✓ Special projects
  ✓ Formal coaching or mentor contracts
  ✓ Educational upgrading
  ✓ Intercompany exchange programs

Identifying and Evaluating Training Courses for Successors

- Consult the in-house training catalog for available courses.
- Determine prices, availability, and waiting lists for external courses.
- Check references for external courses by contacting previous attendees.
- Develop "learning contracts" for informal training, coaching, or mentoring relationships.
- Ensure that succession candidates meet prerequisites for external courses, university programs, or professional upgrading.
- Consider a customized in-house program for succession candidates with common skill gaps.

Calculating Costs and Creating a Budget

- A budget for succession training includes:
  ✓ Course costs
  ✓ Travel and accommodation costs to out-of-town courses
  ✓ Subscriptions to professional journals
  ✓ Specialized equipment needs (e.g., CD-ROM, Internet access, interactive video learning facilities)
  ✓ The costs of time off the job

Implementing the Succession Training Strategy

- Set deadlines for training that addresses high-priority gaps.
- Review the training plan annually to ensure it continues to meet business needs.
- Adapt the plan annually to meet new and emerging corporate priorities.
- Confirm budget approval for succession training costs annually. This is particularly important for long-term strategies.

- Set formal feedback guidelines for coaches and mentors to monitor progress and make recommendations.
- Create opportunities for succession candidates to practice and implement new skills.
- Keep abreast of new courses and lower-cost training options, and amend the training plan accordingly.
- Involve succession candidates in realistic self-assessment exercises after each important training component.
- Determine key learning outcomes for each training component, and monitor these outcomes rigorously.

Team Building Among Participants in the Classroom

T he degree to which participants feel comfortable with and rely on other participants at a course will greatly influence the degree of participation, the quality of discussion, and the opportunity for follow-up and networking after the course to discuss training outcomes. Whether participants know each other or not, there are many techniques that can create conditions for effective team dynamics.

- Pair people up, and have partners introduce each other.
- Include some informal information in the introductions (e.g., most famous person he or she has met). People tend to remember this information more readily than titles and experience.
- Do some research about business backgrounds and experience levels before the training. Emphasize similarities within the group in your introductory comments.
- Repeat informal introductions after the lunch break with another topic (e.g., worst-boss story).
- Total up the number of years of business experience in the room. This emphasizes the whole rather than the parts.
- Mix up the composition of breakout groups during the day to encourage as much interaction as possible.
- Hand out "Bravo!" cards that participants can give to one another when someone has made a helpful suggestion or given a thoughtful answer.
- Seat participants at small, round tables to encourage discussion and teamwork.
- Involve the group in setting break times, suggesting restaurants, and determining incentives for active participation.
- Give out a prize, such as a recent business book, to the partici-

pant who admits to the biggest gaffes in applying the learning principles being taught.

- Take a group picture, and distribute it to all participants at the end of the course.
- Compile a list of addresses and telephone numbers for everyone in the group.
- Have participants autograph each other's diplomas.
- Be sensitive to participants who are not contributing or are distancing themselves from the group. Chat with them at breaks to get a sense of their personal style; use that information to help integrate them into classroom discussions.
- Use self-assessment tools before or during the course, and report on overall trends. Emphasize what is common to the group rather than the differences.
- Play a video that has some humorous insights. A good group chuckle can diffuse tension.
- Above all, avoid the possibility that the group will unite against a poorly prepared or unprofessional facilitator.

Team Development Strategies

Team development is best incorporated into training programs when the organization is committed to creating and/or maintaining a team culture and when team building contributes to the achievement of the training outcomes.

- Team development includes:
  - ✓ Team problem-solving tasks
  - ✓ Team learning activities
- To design team-development activities:
  - ✓ Establish the outcomes to be achieved.
  - ✓ Indicate the steps in the process.
  - ✓ Indicate the time and, where appropriate, resources available.
  - ✓ Include the above information on a task sheet to hand out to each participant at the beginning of the task.
  - ✓ Preset the teams with between five and seven members.
  - ✓ Mix the team membership to ensure a variety of resources.
- To begin the team-development activity:
  - ✓ Hand out the task sheets.
  - ✓ Review the outcomes, the steps in the process, and the time line.
  - ✓ Let the teams do their work. Do not intervene in their process.
- Debrief the results:
  - ✓ At the end of the activity, call time, and ask everyone to stop.
  - ✓ Debrief the results from each of the teams. Where possible, record these results on a flip chart for comparison.
  - ✓ Lead a brief discussion of the content. Provide "expert" answers, with their rationale, where applicable.
- Debrief the process:
  - ✓ Ask the teams *how* they worked together. Steer clear of sliding back into a discussion of the content.

✓ Ask process questions:
  —How did you arrive at this decision?
  —What process did you use?
  —Did a few people control the discussion?
  —Did some people feel they didn't get a chance to speak?
  —How did you manage your time?
  —How is it that your results are different from those of the other teams'?
✓ State that although everyone had the same amount of time, the same number of people, and the same information, the results are different (if they are). Process—how each team got to the end of the task—is a determining factor.
✓ Introduce a more formal reflection on the team process using a team critique instrument.
- Team-critique instruments include such items as:
  ✓ Objective setting and planning
  ✓ Quality of listening
  ✓ Levels of participation
  ✓ Use of time
  ✓ Managing disagreement
  ✓ Decision making
- The team critique:
  ✓ Team-critique instruments are completed individually and then discussed by the whole team.
  ✓ Team members come to common agreement on the ratings of each item.
  ✓ Team members list specific improvements for each item. These improvements can then be applied to the next activity.
  ✓ The facilitator is usually not involved in these discussions.
- Once teams have completed their critiques, team members are invited to share what they've learned with the larger group. This discussion allows the facilitator to build in further team development theory.

Tools for Training: High Tech

Present information during training using a variety of high-tech methods to strengthen understanding and retention.

- The decision to develop or purchase a particular training tool requires a needs analysis that identifies:
  - ✓ The number of employees who will benefit from the training subject matter
  - ✓ The budget
  - ✓ How quickly the tool can be acquired
  - ✓ The amount of time the organization can invest in developing or customizing the training application
  - ✓ The shelf-life of the training principles—that is, whether the material will become outdated as procedures and processes change
  - ✓ The compatibility of your organization's operating systems with specific multimedia applications
- In addition to specific requirements and limitations, there are general considerations that go into making the decision:
  - ✓ The computer literacy of the learners
  - ✓ The availability of and access to networks and computers at different locations
  - ✓ Incentives for employees to use technology-based tools
  - ✓ Managers' availability to discuss and reinforce training principles and skills gained by using training tools.
  - ✓ The likelihood that employees will use self-study tools (consider the current utilization rate for self-study books and videos)
  - ✓ The complexity of the material and training principles for specific courses
  - ✓ The prerequisite training or experience required for certain lessons
- The three tools most often used to support or replace classroom training are:

- ✓ Videoconferencing
- ✓ Interactive multimedia applications
- ✓ Computer-based training
- No matter which training aid you are using, its effectiveness will be enhanced if you:
  - ✓ Use one visual to convey one short message.
  - ✓ Ensure that the visual and verbal messages work in tandem.
  - ✓ Present the messages in a logical order.
  - ✓ See that the operation of the props or visual aid equipment does not interfere with the message being conveyed.
  - ✓ Ensure that gimmickry does not overshadow the message.

Videoconferencing

- The advantages of videoconferencing are:
  - ✓ Reduced travel and accommodation costs for trainees at multiple locations
  - ✓ The opportunity to discuss issues and ask questions
  - ✓ The opportunity to assess participants' ease with the lessons and pace the training accordingly
- The disadvantages of videoconferencing are:
  - ✓ Limitations on the number of participants who can be accommodated at any one location
  - ✓ Reduced interaction among participants
  - ✓ Unease that many participants feel when speaking to a screen
  - ✓ Equipment and facilities that are often unreliable
- Videoconferencing works best when:
  - ✓ Lessons are short (1–2 hours).
  - ✓ Lessons are supported with comprehensive materials for use during and after the session.
  - ✓ The facilitator is at ease with long-distance videoconferencing and has experience in using the medium.
  - ✓ The teaching principles do not rely on small group exercises, which create periods of silence and generally reduce the energy level.

Multimedia Training

- The advantages of interactive multimedia training are:
  - ✓ Participants have flexibility in scheduling training time.
  - ✓ Training can be scheduled around operating requirements.
  - ✓ Trainees can learn at their own pace and review difficult lessons as required.
  - ✓ Trainees can monitor their progress by answering multiple-choice questions.
  - ✓ Managers can get accurate feedback about the use of the tools and trainees' proficiency levels.
  - ✓ Training costs can be reduced because there are no costs for facilitators and travel.
- The disadvantages of using interactive multimedia training are:
  - ✓ Design, development, customization, and installation costs are often high when measured against the intended results.
  - ✓ Off-the-shelf programs may not meet unique organization requirements.
  - ✓ The procedures and processes referenced in the training lessons can change over time, rendering a product useless.
  - ✓ There is no opportunity to assess a trainee's commitment to and interest in practicing the new skills.
- Interactive multimedia training works best when:
  - ✓ Trainees have varying degrees of proficiency in the subject matter and can enter the program at their own level.
  - ✓ Questions and answers are built into the program.
  - ✓ The processes and procedures in the material are unlikely to change in a two-year period.
  - ✓ It is difficult to schedule training around operational requirements.
  - ✓ The training material applies to at least 10 percent of the employee population.
  - ✓ The lessons and skills in the program are procedural or technical in nature.
  - ✓ The lessons are divided into two-hour modules.

Computer-Based Training

- The advantages of using computer-based (disk-based) training are these:

- ✓ This is an extremely cost-effective alternative compared to other technology-based tools or classroom training.
- ✓ There is a wide variety of topics available in this format. Employees can customize their professional development plans.
- ✓ Employees can use the disks at home.
- ✓ Employees can set their own pace in learning the material.
- The disadvantages of using computer-based training are:
  - ✓ There is no way to monitor employee proficiency with the new material.
  - ✓ There is no opportunity to practice the skills during the lesson.
  - ✓ Managers may not be familiar with the material if there are many topics available to the employee.
- Computer-based training works best when:
  - ✓ The lessons are short (1–2 hours).
  - ✓ The lessons are intended to support, not replace, more detailed instruction available in other formats.
  - ✓ Employees have participated in recommending the topics.
  - ✓ The topics are general and are unlikely to contradict or contravene current organization practices.

Trainers: Top Ten Tips

$\mathbf{F}$ocusing on key tasks will ensure success in the classroom.

1. *Stick to an agenda*

     Everyone needs a plan. The agenda is the road map that will lead to the achievement of the learning objectives. Discuss and display the agenda, and outline times for each section. Point out where you are from time to time.

2. *Focus on the learning objectives*

     Keep your eye on the ball. If you allow the workshop to stray too far and for too long, you will disappoint participants. Not using the tools on the job will produce no measurable performance improvement—the most important indicator of success.

3. *Train adults as adults*

     The days of show-and-tell are long gone. You need to:
   - Challenge participants.
   - Respect them.
   - Allow them to influence the process and content of the session.
   - Give them the opportunity to learn through self-discovery.
   - Provide a safe learning environment.
   - Give feedback professionally.

4. *Ensure equal participation*

     It is easy to allow the few confident extroverts to dominate discussions. You can ensure that the time is shared equally:
   - Use a round robin, giving everyone the opportunity to comment, one at a time.
   - Avoid eye contact with those who want to continue to dominate the discussion.
   - Ask the quieter people questions directly.

- Privately make people aware of their tendency to domi-
  nate. Ask for their help in drawing others out.
- Thank people for their willingness to contribute, then say,
  "Let's get some other opinions."

5. *Deal with dysfunctional behaviour*

     There is seldom a workshop in which at least one per-
son does not seem disinterested, hostile, or withdrawn.
These behaviors can be ignored only at your peril. In all
cases, intervene whenever the behavior is affecting others in
the workshop:
- Approach the person.
- Make the person aware of your concern.
- Focus on the problem. Do not make a personal attack.
- Listen to any complaints the person may have.
- Offer help, insofar as you may have control over the
  problem.
- Ask for the person's cooperation by appealing to his or
  her maturity.

6. *Give your best*

     People have high expectations for training delivery. You
need to give 100 percent of your enthusiasm and knowledge
to be appreciated. If things aren't going as planned, though,
and you've tried to rectify the situation:
- Don't apologize for any shortfalls. Your participants may
  not even be aware that there is a problem.
- Be assertive in dealing with the problem. Weakness and a
  lack of decisiveness on your part will erode trainees' confidence in the program.

7. *Review the agenda*

     At the end of each day or the beginning of the next day,
review what you have covered. This can be done through:
- A brief summary by you.
- A round robin, asking people to call out one thing that
  they found useful so far.

8. *Listen to the trainees*

     Never work in a vacuum. You ignore participants at
your peril.
- Listen to what they say and how they say it.
- Observe body language. Negative signs may include:
  ✓ Rolling eyes

✓ Avoiding eye contact
✓ Crossed arms and legs
✓ Folding arms behind the head and leaning back
✓ Leaving the room frequently
- When you notice a problem, listen closely to questions so that you can fully answer them. You can do this best by:
  ✓ Rephrasing their questions, to confirm your understanding.
  ✓ Not filling your mind with a rebuttal or even a better idea as someone is speaking.

9. *Provide a safe environment*

People need to practice skills before they can be expected to use them in their work environment. You can create a sense of security by:
- Using humor and self-deprecation.
- Stressing the importance of learning from feedback.
- Being a role model, then inviting feedback on how you are doing.
- Establishing a learning contract that stresses the importance of helping one another through feedback.

10. *Have fun*

People learn best when the environment is relaxed and they are enjoying themselves. This will not detract from the importance of the task at hand. You can help to keep a smile on participants' faces by:
- Telling appropriate jokes.
- Laughing at yourself.
- Illustrating theory with amusing anecdotes.
- Using short activities that are fun.
- Keeping an upbeat tempo.

Training Materials

M aterials are important during and after training. Here are some ideas as to how to make them as effective as possible.

- Bear in mind that the audience will include people who learn best in one of three ways: visual, auditory, and kinesthetic. Your presentation should include all three modalities for maximum impact.
- Decide on the best medium for the visual part of the presentation. The most commonly used media are slides or overheads for a formal presentation or flip charts for an informal presentation. People require about 40 percent less time to grasp a concept with visual aids than with verbal instruction alone.
- If you use slides or overheads:
  - ✓ Keep them short and to the point.
  - ✓ Use one idea per transparency or slide.
  - ✓ Add pictures where possible.
  - ✓ Make sure that letters are large, bold, and legible.
- Develop materials to suit the audience. For example, materials for people with poor literacy should have more pictures and diagrams.
- Materials will be better if they:
  - ✓ Contain one idea per page.
  - ✓ Are written in simple language.
  - ✓ Have lots of space to make notes.
  - ✓ Are interactive, with spaces for people to write answers, do quizzes, and complete checklists.
- You have two choices with regard to materials:
  - ✓ Develop your own.
  - ✓ Buy a ready-made program.

Ready-Made Programs

- Consider buying a packaged program if development costs are high. Avoid packages that:

- ✓ Will date quickly (high-tech subjects are particularly vulnerable).
- ✓ Cannot be customized.
- ✓ Have audiovisuals from a very different industry.
- ✓ Are aimed at a very different audience level.
- ✓ Are made in a foreign country.
- An ideal packaged program:
  - ✓ Can be tried before you commit.
  - ✓ Is recommended by others in your industry.
  - ✓ Lends itself to easy updating.
  - ✓ Can be duplicated without breaking any copyright.

Developing Your Own Materials

- Ensure that your materials include:
  - ✓ A title page
  - ✓ A letter of endorsement from a sponsor, such as the president
  - ✓ A table of contents
  - ✓ Instructions on how to use the manual
  - ✓ The body content
  - ✓ Appropriate appendixes
- In assembling the content for the manual, refer to:
  - ✓ Existing materials
  - ✓ Documents from the work area that the training is being designed for
  - ✓ Human resources professionals who may shed light on any corporate policies that have a bearing on your subject matter
  - ✓ Legal counsel, should the topic be subject to legislation at the local or national level
- The language in your workbook should:
  - ✓ Talk to, never down to, participants.
  - ✓ Be written in a style that is easy to read and conversational in tone.
  - ✓ Make use of clear, short, and familiar words.
  - ✓ Not include words that do not add to the meaning of any sentence.
  - ✓ Be free of jargon.

✓ Have short sentences that contain one thought only.
✓ Use point form wherever possible.
✓ Emphasize key ideas or words by making them bold, italicized, or underlined.
✓ Avoid sexist language or the use of only male pronouns.
✓ Contain lots of white space for trainees to make notes.
✓ Be interspersed with exercises that will allow trainees to document their own ideas or answer a quiz.
✓ Contain lots of diagrams, pictures, and charts.
✓ Contain chapters for each new topic, clearly designated with a chapter opening page.

Training Program Design

Training programs can't be developed in a vacuum. They need to be placed in an organization context and then designed with the specific training needs of the targeted employee(s).

- At the outset of your design efforts:
  - ✓ Speak with managers about the organization's operating environment: the political, economic, social, and technological trends that have an impact on the organization and may give rise to training needs.
  - ✓ Gather information on the organization's short-, medium-, and longer-term objectives to ensure that your training program supports these directions.
  - ✓ Secure your manager's support for the training program, including the funding and the time to develop and deliver the training.
  - ✓ Check the marketplace to see if a program that might meet your needs and objectives already exists. Ask people who might have attended it what they liked about it and any misgivings that they had too.
- Determine whether the training will benefit your customers, internal or external. If it will not, don't waste your time and the organization's money.
- Identify when employees need knowledge, skills, or both. If skills are needed, you will need to incorporate practice into your workshop.
- Plan short sessions rather than one four- or five-day session if the content is highly technical. People retain skills more effectively if you present the training in half-day lessons.
- Learn all you can about your audience:
  - ✓ What they need to know
  - ✓ What they need to do better
  - ✓ Their existing level of performance

- ✓ Their motivation
- ✓ Their literacy
- ✓ If they have any "hot buttons," such as bad experiences in previous training sessions, concerns about downsizing, or low scores in a recent employee satisfaction survey.
- ✓ What previous courses they have taken that relate in some way
- In analyzing training needs:
  - ✓ Identify the tasks that must be done and the skills required to do them.
  - ✓ Check existing job descriptions and vendors' technical manuals for information on these requirements.
  - ✓ Conduct an assessment of the skill levels of the employees doing the job.
  - ✓ Determine the nature of the performance gap between required and existing skills.
  - ✓ Locate existing procedures and check to see if the procedures are still up-to-date.
  - ✓ Review any regulations that apply to procedures or conduct.
  - ✓ Make sure there is a training need rather than other performance deficiencies, such as a poorly designed job, unrealistic expectations, or an attitude problem.
- Set learning objectives. Document them, and later share them with the trainees. Learning objectives should be:
  - ✓ Stated in clear, simple language, using one objective for each sentence.
  - ✓ Listed in a logical order.
- Plan your agenda. This should cover:
  - ✓ Welcome and introductions.
  - ✓ An icebreaker.
  - ✓ Clarification and buy-in to objectives.
  - ✓ Individual training modules.
  - ✓ Breaks.
  - ✓ Questions and answers.
  - ✓ Wrap-up.
  - ✓ Evaluation.
- Before rolling the training out to everyone:
  - ✓ Test the materials on a pilot group.
  - ✓ Select the pilot group from a cross-section of your potential

audience. Be sure to include people who will be forthright and objective in their feedback.

- Time your training so that it is not too early or too late for your objective. If you schedule your session too far in advance of when people need to use the skills, they will forget what you have taught. Training after they have started will require some unlearning since they may have developed bad habits already.
- To set training priorities:
  - ✓ Determine the impact of the training need on the organization's ability to attain its objectives or comply with legislation.
  - ✓ Identify the impact on the individual employee's ability to succeed at the job.
  - ✓ Assess the cost-to-benefit of the training effort.
- When developing the training content, keep it focused:
  - ✓ Establish clear objectives for the training by completing the sentence: "At the end of this program, the employee(s) will be able to . . ."
  - ✓ Prepare a high-level outline or blueprint of the program, setting out major content areas or modules, the training objectives for each module, and the expected outcomes of the training.
  - ✓ Select the most suitable combination of instructional techniques: self-study, lecture, one-to-one coaching, video, simulations, case studies, computer-based training, hands-on practice, or interactive learning.
  - ✓ If you use your own design, assemble a small team, including one or two employees from the group to be trained, to validate the training materials before you deliver the program.
  - ✓ Consult subject matter experts for accuracy.

Train-the-Trainer Sessions

Whether you are an external training provider or an in-house training professional, from time to time, you may train others in the delivery of a training session in order to increase the pool of available trainers for key programs.

There are three important responsibilities for train-the-trainer sessions:

1. Selection of participants
2. Preparation of materials
3. Conducting the session

Selecting Participants

- Seek nominations from managers about staff who have experience in presenting to groups and some knowledge in the subject area, and are regarded as champions or role models.
- Interview potential trainers to get a sense of their style and commitment to the project. It is better to disappoint one potential trainer than to disappoint trainees whose learning was compromised by a poor facilitator.
- Do not rule out nominees with no previous training experience. Consider other related experience, such as sales presentations, community relations, and experience in chairing meetings.

Preparing Materials

- A facilitator's binder should contain:
  ✓ Complete participants' manual
  ✓ Comprehensive facilitator notes

✓ Guidelines and articles about effective facilitation techniques

✓ Complete set of overheads

✓ Complete set of handouts

✓ Copies of videos used during the training session

✓ Evaluation form used for the course

- In order to make the facilitator's guide user friendly:

  ✓ Use symbols to denote *flip chart, overhead,* and *handouts,* as they occur in the session.

  ✓ Use only the right-hand side of the manual for printed information. Leave the left-hand side blank for notes.

  ✓ Integrate copies of overheads and handouts as they occur during the session, so that users do not need to flip back and forth in the manual.

  ✓ Include suggested responses for all exercises. Make the list as comprehensive as possible.

  ✓ Include information and background data that will help facilitators deal with some potentially difficult teaching principles.

  ✓ Lay out the manual as attractively as possible, and use bold type so that the facilitator can see it easily at a comfortable distance.

  ✓ Use different colors to delineate the facilitator's role and the participants' activities.

  ✓ Use well-marked dividers for each separate lesson or exercise.

Conducting the Session

- Review the key teaching principles and anticipated outcomes informally with participants before walking them through the manual.

- Discuss the group's experiences as trainees (best and worst experiences) as an aid to understanding the trainees' perspectives.

- Review the manual and the lessons in digestible chunks, and debrief facilitators after each section.

- Conduct all role plays and exercises so that facilitators appreciate the impact these will have on trainees.

- After a comprehensive review of the manual, assign facilitators to deliver individual sections to the group. Allow them enough time to prepare the lesson plans and to rehearse.
- Be constructive in debriefing facilitators about delivery glitches.
- Debrief each facilitator in private about his or her facilitator style and technique.
- Videotape some practice sessions, and let facilitators review their own performance.
- Review evaluations from previous courses with the group to understand some major concerns and highlights of previous courses.
- Set up a hot-line so that facilitators can contact you with urgent issues during a course they are conducting.
- Send updates, amendments, and tips to facilitators during the course delivery schedule.
- Prepare a list of facilitator names and contact details so they can share advice with each other after conducting the course solo.

Trends: What's Hot and What's Not

Training trends keep pace with the ebb and flow of management theories, changes in information technology, and social and demographic shifts in the market place.

What's Hot: Trends That Have Gained Momentum Over the Past Five Years

- *Diversity and sensitivity training.* This training equips employees to deal with differences among themselves, as well as with changing demographics in the customer base.
- *Creating a learning organization.* This is a process, not a program, that encourages continuous learning in and outside the classroom.
- *Core competencies.* Many organizations are defining key success criteria (both hard and soft skills) and tailoring training programs to teach and underscore these essential skills.
- *360° feedback.* This performance evaluation system uses input from all employee levels in assessing performance. Training is an important factor in helping employees to use the process effectively.
- *Succession planning.* Talented people are more mobile than ever, and companies are designing individual professional development plans to retain high-performing staff to fill future executive vacancies.
- *Measuring training's effectiveness.* No longer can companies afford to train people simply because it's "the right thing to do." Any training investment must have measurable outcomes. Companies are finding new ways to measure the effectiveness of their training dollars.
- *Mentoring.* Formal and informal programs are gaining popularity as a means of reinforcing individual employee develop-

ment and encouraging senior managers to act as coaches and role models.
- *Self-directed learning*. This learning process requires individuals to take more responsibility for their own learning. The individuals are empowered to decide what they need to learn and when and how to do it

What's Not: Trends That Have Lost Momentum in the Past Five Years

- *Empowerment*. Empowerment is a long-term change in attitude, not a course. Companies often couldn't follow through on promises made in training courses.
- *Total quality management*. Many companies seriously underestimated the time, energy, and costs of producing results, and they consequently abandoned the process before any lasting improvements were made.
- *Vision and values*. Turnover in executive teams and changing market conditions have left many employees uncertain about the ongoing commitment to a rigid set of statements. In many cases, cynicism set in when operating practices ran counter to values.
- *Large corporate training departments*. Many companies have come to rely on just-in-time training and outsourcing as business circumstances changed faster than corporate training agendas.
- *Classroom training*. The availability of new forms of self-directed learning using modern telecommunications and computer technologies is challenging the notion that classroom training is the best option for learning.

Tuition Reimbursement: Getting the Most From a Program

M any companies offer tuition reimbursement programs that subsidize the costs of continuing education for employees. Three key benefits accrue to companies that offer these programs:

1. Upgrading the skills of their labor force
2. Providing incentives for employees to remain with the company
3. Attracting new employees by offering tuition reimbursement as part of a comprehensive benefits package

Although there is always a concern that employees who take part in tuition reimbursement programs may leave the company, experience and research demonstrate that companies that offer the programs gain in the long term by their demonstrated commitment to employee development.

- Most tuition reimbursement programs have common eligibility criteria:
  - ✓ Courses are offered at recognized educational institutes.
  - ✓ Successful completion of the course results in accreditation toward a certificate, diploma, or degree.
  - ✓ Reimbursement is contingent on successful completion of the program.
  - ✓ Employees must attend courses outside regular business hours.
- Some important differences in administering tuition reimbursement programs among companies are:
  - ✓ The amount of funding available for tuition reimbursement

- ✓ Variable levels of reimbursement (partial versus full reimbursement)
- ✓ Maximum levels of reimbursement per employee
- ✓ Reimbursement of course-related expenses (travel costs, books, materials)
- ✓ Approval responsibility
- These guidelines will help to generate maximum returns and meaningful outcomes for the company and its employees:
  - ✓ Be flexible. Review the program annually, and be prepared to consider unusual cases.
  - ✓ Solicit employee input about program guidelines and administration.
  - ✓ Involve an employee's manager in decision making and recommendations about an employee's request. This reinforces the manager's role as a coach.
  - ✓ Generate publicity about the program to reinforce the company's commitment to employee development.
  - ✓ Review the program guidelines to make sure that certain groups aren't precluded from participating (e.g., single mothers who require babysitters, disabled employees who need special equipment).
  - ✓ Maintain a reference library with catalogs and calendars from local colleges and universities.
  - ✓ Research distance-learning opportunities.
  - ✓ Profile employee success stories in company newsletters.
  - ✓ Develop creative ways for employees to "pay back" the company (e.g., participating in public relations events, charity commitments, tutoring and coaching assignments with other employees).
  - ✓ Include information about the tuition reimbursement program in the orientation program.
  - ✓ Allocate a companywide budget for tuition reimbursement rather than individual departments so that all interested employees can access the fund.
  - ✓ Review usage statistics regularly to determine if some areas or departments rarely use the program, and find out why.
  - ✓ Don't approve long-term courses all at once. Do semiannual or annual approvals.
- Follow up with employees when they complete courses. Have employees describe how the course has benefited the company as well as them.

Videos: Using Them to Their Best Advantage

Video can be a wonderful tool to use in teaching, but its value and effectiveness can be diminished by incorrect use.

- Instead of showing videos in their entirety, show clips. Pick a scene to model behavior or the opposite. Ask people what they liked or how they might do things differently.
- Develop a case study, and use a clip to illustrate one aspect.
- Make videos available to people afterward in the resource library, should they want to review the materials, show them to colleagues, or see the whole program.
- Determine the appropriate use for the video:
  - ✓ What am I trying to achieve through showing this video? What are the desired learning outcomes?
  - ✓ Where might this video best be placed?
    - —To initiate discussion?
    - —To summarize learning?
    - —As part of a case study?
  - ✓ Integrate the video into the training design.
  - ✓ Where appropriate, set out the desired learning outcomes in advance of viewing the video.
  - ✓ Design questions related to the video, for response by individuals or teams.
- Always:
  - ✓ View the video in advance of the program to ensure your own thorough knowledge of its key points.
  - ✓ Check video clarity, color, and sound just before the workshop.
  - ✓ Beware of videos where fashions or verbal expressions are considerably out of date; trainees will be easily distracted by these discrepancies.

- When considering renting or purchasing a video, keep in mind:
  - ✓ There are excellent previewing services available. Use them rather than relying on catalog summaries.
  - ✓ Look in your local library for low-cost alternatives for borrowing.
  - ✓ Send out an SOS to your organization asking if there are any good videos available on a specific topic. Many managers have a wide selection of videos sitting unused in cabinets.
  - ✓ Other organizations you deal with may have good videos that you can borrow in exchange for some other service.
  - ✓ Do your math when deciding to rent or buy. If you intend to use the video for several sessions, it is usually more cost-effective to buy it outright.

Producing a Video In-House

- You may have the facilities to produce a video in-house, even with a limited budget.
  In-house video production for training works best for:
  - ✓ Executive messages (including an endorsement of a training program)
  - ✓ A question-and-answer session that discusses some teaching points in the course
  - ✓ Demonstration of equipment repair techniques
  - ✓ A visual tour of a plant or production facility
- Making an in-house video without the benefit of a professional scriptwriter can be accomplished by one of these alternatives:
  - ✓ Write the initial drafts yourself, and have a professional edit your text.
  - ✓ Send someone from your organization for training to learn the basics.
- Getting time from a senior person to endorse your program can be difficult. You will make your task easier if you:
  - ✓ Choose to work with people who are committed to the message, even though they may not be at the highest level.

- ✓ Prepare them in advance of the time requirement, with the understanding that seldom is the first take satisfactory.
- ✓ Get their input into the content, so that they appear genuinely happy to make whatever pitch it is.
- ✓ Prepare the set beforehand to make sure that little time is wasted when they arrive.
- A lengthy speech filmed with one camera can be improved by:
  - ✓ Suggesting to the executive that it be edited to include highlights.
  - ✓ Interspersing the view of the executive with clips of people and places that might illustrate his or her points visually.
- Make use of professional actors if:
  - ✓ You need to save time.
  - ✓ You have the budget.
  - ✓ Your organization is fairly large and the person you are portraying is not well known.
  - ✓ The job you are showing is done by a number of people.
  - ✓ The topic is generic and applies throughout the organization (e.g., health and safety).
- *Caution:* Mixing professional actors with staff is rarely a good idea because the presence of the professionals will intimidate your employees. You can use in-house people and have a professional narrator do commentaries and background voices.
- The choice of where to shoot will be influenced by:
  - ✓ The budget
  - ✓ The ability to build or create authentic scenes away from work
  - ✓ The convenience of having all the equipment in one place and not having to travel from place to place
  - ✓ The possibility of interference of people and noises on-site

The Year 2000: Training's Role and Trainer Requirements

As the business environment changes, so will the role that training and trainers play to meet corporate challenges.

- Here are some important new dimensions of the internal customer. They are:
  - ✓ More demanding
  - ✓ More knowledgeable
  - ✓ Able to access information much easier
  - ✓ Fiscally accountable
  - ✓ Accountable to a variety of people and levels
  - ✓ More aware of competitive strategies
- Here are some important ways that the employee configuration in organizations has changed and continues to evolve:
  - ✓ More diverse in interests and expectations
  - ✓ Greater demographic diversity
  - ✓ Less loyal to employers
  - ✓ More threatened about employment security
  - ✓ More diverse learning styles
  - ✓ Stronger computer literacy
- Emerging trainer competencies will include:
  - ✓ Multimedia selection and design
  - ✓ Financial analysis and budget skills
  - ✓ Ability to outsource successfully
  - ✓ Management of diversity
  - ✓ Delivery mode analysis
  - ✓ Analysis of the relationship between training and the bottom line
- Emerging training trends in the workplace include:
  - ✓ Strategic partnerships and outsourcing
  - ✓ Distance learning
  - ✓ Self-paced learning

- ✓ Self-directed learning
- ✓ Peer training
- Trainers can prepare themselves for new and important challenges in the workplace in the following ways:
  - ✓ Learn about learning theories.
  - ✓ Become proficient on the Internet.
  - ✓ Get 360° feedback about personal consulting skills and styles.
  - ✓ Gain sophisticated business analysis skills.
  - ✓ Join corporate task forces.
  - ✓ Attend training conferences for networking and research.
  - ✓ Practice pragmatism about fads and fashions in behavioral theory.
  - ✓ Meet with the external customer as often as possible, and continuously assess their needs.
  - ✓ Understand the change process through a variety of models and theories.
  - ✓ Understand annual reports.
  - ✓ Understand competitors' strategies.
  - ✓ Learn how to cost products and services.
  - ✓ Gain multimedia expertise.

Category Index

Buying

Alternatives to Training
Budgeting for Training
Budgets: Building a Case for More Training Dollars
Computer-Based Training
Consultants
Cost Controls
Facilities: How to Choose Them
Methodology: Choosing the Right One
Outsourcing
Requests for Proposal
Trends: What's Hot and What's Not

Conducting

Case Studies
Coaching
Conducting a Training Session
Difficult Behavior During Training
Diversity in the Classroom
Facilitator Tips: The Top Ten
Facilitator Turnoffs: The Top Ten
Feedback From the Trainer to Participants
Flip Chart Do's and Don'ts
Games in Training
Humor
Icebreakers
Impact in the Classroom
Internet and Intranet
Keeping Trainees in the Classroom
Learning Contracts
Lesson Plan Development
Mentoring
Nervousness: Overcoming Butterflies
On-the-Job Training
Orientation Programs
Outdoor Training
Overhead Do's and Don'ts
Participation in Workshops
Peer Training
Presentation Skills
Product Training
Resistance to Training
Role-Play: Design and Conduct
Simulations
Team Building Among Participants in the Classroom
Team Development Strategies
Videos: Using Them to Their Best Advantage

Sending

Conferences and Seminars
Learning Contracts
Minimizing Time off the Job
Needs Analysis: Using 360° Feedback
Product Training

Tuition Reimbursement: Getting the Most
   From a Program

Supporting   Career Planning Programs
Coaching
Internet and Intranet
Learning Organizations
Mentoring
Professional Associations: A Checklist for
   Selecting and Joining
Record Keeping
Resource Centers
Rewards and Recognition
Self-Directed Learning
Train-the-Trainer Sessions
Trends: What's Hot and What's Not
Tuition Reimbursement: Getting the Most
   From a Program

Index